"Imagine a classroom in which your students read to l......... ...e world, then study how texts are made so that they can write ι. ᴄnange the world. In this book, Dr. Jessica Singer Early shows you how to teach next generation genres so that your students can become better readers and writers while producing op-eds, profiles, podcasts, and more."

—**Tanya Baker**, director, national programs at National Writing Project

"Jessica Singer Early's *Next Generation Genres* gives us such relevant, practical techniques for thinking about teaching writing to others and to ourselves. It is a refreshing frame for reengaging our students in the purpose and multifaceted practices of the craft."

—**Tonya B. Perry**, PhD, professor and executive director of GEAR UP Alabama and Red Mountain Writing Project

"Jessica Singer Early invites teachers to move beyond 'school writing'—those tired, often formulaic essays and general reports that have no existence (or readership) outside school walls. Instead, she makes a compelling case to bring in real genres that use a range of digital tools and that have a civic purpose."

—**Thomas Newkirk**, professor emeritus, University of New Hampshire, and author of *Writing Unbound: How Fiction Transforms Student Writers* (Heinemann)

"In *Next Generation Genres: Teaching Writing for Civic Engagement*, Jessica Singer Early demystifies many of the moves professional writers make so adolescent composers can try them, too. Each chapter is constructed with workshop tips, tools for digital spaces, ways to adapt and extend, model texts, sample assignments, guiding questions, and student results. Each provides tools for teaching students how to read as writers in the National Writing Project method. The best part, however, is that the genres highlighted by Early (turning point essays, artist statements, PSAs, infographics, op-eds, profile essays, podcasts, and proposals) promote opportunities for students to make the world a better place. *Next Generation Genres* positions middle and high school students to join writing communities as agentive and purposeful thinkers. It is the perfect book to mentor effective practices for teaching writing. I can't wait to share its brilliance with educators across the country."

—**Bryan Ripley Crandall**, associate professor of English education and director of the Connecticut Writing Project, School of Education and Human Development, Fairfield University

"With insights and inspiration for moving students into modes that matter for life beyond school, Jessica Singer Early brings her sensibilities as an English teacher and as a National Writing Project site director to her book, *Next Generation Genres*. Through eight different styles of writing, she provides teachers with a clear rationale, practical steps, technology tips, and student examples for each. She offers multiple approaches to renew the academic essay and invites students into multimodal compositions through image, audio, and video as well. Early's deep knowledge of pedagogy and her own humility as a writer combine to honor her readers' experiences as educators themselves while bringing them a timely, practical, and positive approach to the teaching of writing in secondary classrooms."

—**Troy Hicks**, professor of English and education, Central Michigan University, director of the Chippewa River Writing Project, and author of *Creating Confident Writers* (W. W. Norton)

NEXT
GENERATION
GENRES

NORTON BOOKS IN EDUCATION

NEXT GENERATION GENRES

TEACHING WRITING
FOR CIVIC AND ACADEMIC ENGAGEMENT

JESSICA SINGER EARLY

Norton Professional Books

An Imprint of W. W. Norton & Company
Celebrating a Century of Independent Publishing

This book is intended as a general information resource for teachers and school administrators. It is not a substitute for appropriate training or supervision. Standards of practice and protocol vary in different educational settings and change over time. No technique or recommendation is guaranteed to be effective in all circumstances, and neither the publisher nor the author can guarantee the complete accuracy, efficacy, or appropriateness of any particular recommendation in every respect or in all settings or circumstances.

The author is not a lawyer, and nothing contained in this book should be construed as legal advice. For advice about how to comply with the various copyright and privacy laws and requirements that are implicated in creating written and audiovisual works and how to prepare appropriate permission documents, please consult your school or district legal counsel or another attorney with relevant expertise.

Any URLs displayed in this book link or refer to websites that existed as of press time. The publisher is not responsible for, and should not be deemed to endorse or recommend, any website other than its own or any app or other content that it did not create. The author, also, is not responsible for any third-party material.

For information about permission to reproduce selections from this book, write to Permissions, W. W. Norton & Company, Inc., 500 Fifth Avenue, New York, NY 10110

For information about special discounts for bulk purchases, please contact W. W. Norton Special Sales at specialsales@wwnorton.com or 800-233-4830

Manufacturing by Versa Press
Production manager: Gwen Cullen

ISBN: 9781324019688 (pbk)

W. W. Norton & Company, Inc., 500 Fifth Avenue, New York, NY 10110
www.wwnorton.com

W. W. Norton & Company Ltd., 15 Carlisle Street, London W1D 3BS

1 2 3 4 5 6 7 8 9 0

For Jake, Lucca, Jax, Pippin, and Xavi

Contents

Acknowledgments

This book would not be possible without the collaboration and support of incredible doctoral students and writing project teacher leaders at Arizona State University: Ginette Rossi, Heather O'Loughlin, Justin Scholes, Amber Curlee, Michelle Glerum, Andrea Rivers, Rosanne Orta, Ashley Yap, and Monica Baldonado-Ruiz. My gratitude to two brilliant editors at Norton: Sarah Touborg, who believed in my work from the beginning, and Carol Collins, who helped me shape this project. Charles Bazerman and Tom Newkirk, thank you for being wonderful mentors and influences on my work for all these years. Thank you to the scholars, leaders, and changemakers in the National Writing Project who support the teaching and research of writing across this country. I am especially grateful for Tanya Baker, my sounding board for work and life, and Dave Beck, who keeps me distracted enough to write with a steady stream of soccer updates. Thank you to Kris Ratcliffe for being a champion of my work and for the work of others at ASU. Jake, thank you for being my best friend, the best father, and the best pizza maker. A special thanks to Jax, who let me take up a corner of his bedroom for a year during the pandemic. I wrote this book beside him while he did fourth grade online. You can have your desk back now, Jax.

Author's Note

Although I am not a lawyer and this book is not a legal treatise, there are a couple of legal issues that need to be called out when talking about teaching writing to students: copyright and privacy. While it is obviously very unlikely that anyone would assert a legal claim based on an elementary or high school student's class presentation, the chances of such a claim might increase if that student published her work outside the school context, for example, in a local newspaper, which is something that, in the book, I recommend you encourage your students to do. Works created by students in higher education also may be publicized outside their classrooms. Moreover, the writing and presentation skills that this book seeks to help you teach are skills that I hope your students will use long after they graduate from your school, in their professional education and work.

The following points are intended only to flag certain considerations that you and your students should be aware of. Your schools and school districts may have policies that address these issues, so you should always be aware and mindful of such policies when assigning projects that may raise these issues. You also may want to consult individual treatises and practitioners in these areas for further guidance. Students should be encouraged to consult their teachers, and teachers should consult their school administrators to determine whether their schools or school districts have policies that address any or all of these potential legal problems.

Copyright

Under US copyright law, copying, distributing copies of, creating derivative works of (adapting), publicly displaying, and publicly performing someone else's work without permission generally constitute copyright infringement. To give just a few examples, a photo, text from an article, a video, a graphic image (such as a cartoon character), a sound recording (a recording of a song), or a set of song lyrics each constitutes a "work" for purposes of copyright. Subject to certain exceptions that are not relevant here, digitally transmitting someone else's sound recording also constitutes infringement.

Liability for copyright infringement is what is called strict liability: If you use someone's work without permission, it is not a defense that you may not have known that you were doing something unlawful. In certain cases, if someone is found to have infringed someone else's copyright, the copyright owner may recover substantial monetary damages.

There are some defenses to infringement. One of those is "fair use" defense. Fair use is often misunderstood. "Fair use" does not mean any use that the user thinks is fair and it does not mean any and every use by a student. The copyright law lists four nonexclusive factors that a court must apply to analyze whether a use is "fair use": the nature and character of the use in question, the nature of the infringed work (certain kinds of works get less protection), the amount and substantiality of the portion of the work that was used relative to the infringed work as a whole, and the effect on the actual or potential market for the use (in other words, if everyone did what the infringer did, what effect would that have on the market for the work). For purposes of this book, it is enough to say that the fair use defense does not give students a "get out of jail free" card, even if the risk of an infringement claim is low.

Credit (attribution) does not equal permission. It would not be a defense to a copyright infringement claim for a student to say that they gave credit to the creator of the work that they used.

Many online sites offer free photos, graphics, and other works. But many of those sites do not promise that they actually have the right to offer those works to the public, even if they assert that their works are "properly attributed." That means that if a student uses such a work, even though the student thinks that they are using the work lawfully because they obtained the work from that site, the owner of the copyright in that work still could claim that the student's use infringed their copyright, and the site would not necessarily have any legal responsibility for having made the work available in the first place.

Use of photos from online sources carries a particularly high risk, because many photographers watermark their works and engage law firms and other services to police the Internet to see whether anyone is using their works without permission. Usually, once one of those law firms or services spots a work that appears to be in use without permission, they will send a letter demanding the payment of what may be very high fees under the threat of a lawsuit, and these claims can be extremely difficult and expensive to defend. Your students should be taught to read the terms of use on any site where they are looking for free images or other works to use in their assignments, especially if there is a chance that those assignments will be submitted for publication outside of their school.

The use of song lyrics also carries a special degree of risk. The companies that control the rights in song lyrics are known to police uses (including those that might be considered "fair use" under the Copyright Act) very vigorously, and to demand high fees for unlicensed use of those lyrics.

Even works that are offered online for use under a "Creative Commons" license can come with restrictions. For example, a Creative Commons license may prohibit commercial use of the work or may require that credit be given to the creator each time the work is displayed. Your students should know to read the Creative Commons license associated with any work they use and make sure that they are complying with its terms.

Privacy

A student who is writing a profile or an essay about someone they know, or is even just interviewing someone for an article or essay, should get permission from their subject to describe them and whatever events the student wants to write about, and to publish the piece wherever the student intends to publish it. Written permission is optimal, but if a student cannot get, or does not feel comfortable asking for, written permission, it may be sufficient for the student to record herself telling the subject that she wants to interview the subject for an article about [x] that she intends to publish. If it is possible that the student will want to submit the article for publication outside of school, the student should be sure to mention that in asking for permission in the first place.

If an interview subject does not want to be identified in a student's written work, the student can try to disguise their identity. Just changing the subject's name may not enough. People can be identified by many attributes in addition to their name: their physical appearance, the city or neighborhood where they live, their job, and their family, just by way of example.

Introduction

When I taught high school English in an urban school in Portland, Oregon, one of my students once asked if she had written a narrative or an argument. I didn't know how to answer. I thought I had assigned students to write a narrative, but when she asked this, I realized my instructions and what I had provided as mentor texts seemed as if they could count as either narrative or expository. This stopped me in my tracks. How could a piece of writing be more than one mode? Until that moment, a narrative was a narrative in my mind, and an argument was an argument.

At that time, my school district and state required that I cover narrative, creative and poetic, argumentative, and expository modes. I had had very little training in the teaching of writing. I organized my writing curriculum around these categories because they were the categories required of me, and they made sense to manage my curricular schedule. I taught a narrative at the beginning of the year and then moved to creative and poetic and then on to argument and, finally, expository. I taught these as distinctly separate forms of writing.

While I may have been covering my bases in terms of what was required of me by my school, district, and state, I kept getting caught on the fact that writing I read in the world and the texts I brought in to serve as models for my students didn't fit neatly into these tidy categories. For example, I used as a model text for my narrative essay writing unit an essay entitled "La Tortierra" by Patricia Preciado Martin (1996), which describes the author making tortillas with her mother. The beautiful story shares a tradition passed from one generation to another. It is a story about cooking, but also identity and culture. Besides sharing a narrative memory, the piece also teaches the reader how the author's mother makes tortillas from scratch. One of the things I love most about this text is how Martin provides rules the mother maintains for being in her kitchen and shares the steps her mother takes to make homemade tortillas. As I read this piece to my students, I kept thinking, "Isn't this narrative also expository? It tells the story of memory and teaches the reader how to make tortillas as the mother makes them. Could it be two modes simultaneously and, if so, how do I teach that?" I realized that using modes as a framework and guide for thinking about, teaching, and organizing the teaching of writing was limiting the way I thought about and taught writing. Using modes as an organizing framework and approach did not match the ways writing works in the world.

Why Genre?

Although it felt like it to me, this was not a new revelation. Composition scholars have theorized, researched, and taught about writing beyond modes for years at the college level. In popular parlance, "genre" means fiction categories such as literary, mystery, science fiction, or romance. In the field of writing studies, it refers to forms of writing created to communicate within specific contexts and for particular audiences and purposes. Written genres typically have common features or elements that are repeated or expected in their use. Genre is a useful framework for thinking about the teaching of writing for the simple reason that it provides a straightforward platform for understanding the social conventions and expectations of writing forms. We write as social beings within shared spaces and for authentic audiences and purposes. We write to communicate ideas, learn, make sense of lived experiences, and access new pathways and opportunities. We also write because we become deeply invested in issues and ideas or social worlds that we want to be a part of, influence, or even change.

Genre theory is based on the understanding that writing is a social practice that reflects certain norms and expectations created within and for a community. Communities continually set, maintain, and shift expectations for the discourse practices within their social context, and, in turn, a genre or set of genres emerge. For example, attorneys learn to write legal briefs using the written conventions and text features that are expected by the court and the legal community. School administrators write evaluations of their teaching staff based on in-person teaching observations. These evaluation letters are an agreed-upon written genre with certain shared characteristics. Their production is part of the practice of being a principal and receiving them is part of being a public school teacher. In college, a wide range of genres are practiced within each discipline, and these continually evolve to fit new expectations, technologies, forms of communication, and social demands. A genre approach to thinking about and teaching writing had not entered the teaching of secondary writing when I began my career years ago. Even today, the use of modes—argument, narrative, and others—persists as a guiding framework for the teaching of secondary writing.

Although the use of modes persists in secondary writing classrooms, the past thirty years have brought about significant changes in the ways writing is produced, used, and shared. Many of these developments have taken place as part of the onset of advanced technologies, increased access to the internet, the evolution of digital and multimodal forms of literacy, and the economic and social demands of globalization. These changes have led the National Council of Teachers of English (NCTE) and the International Literacy Association (ILA), among other leading literacy organizations, to issue position statements on the importance of teaching writing to address and reflect the complexities and intricacies of 21st-century literacy practices. These policy statements recommend that teachers of writing:

1. provide more time for students to write for diverse audiences and purposes.
2. connect writing to reading.
3. provide clear instruction on strategies and approaches for how to write.
4. take students through a writing process (e.g., invention, drafting, revision, and making public).
5. write to share cultural and linguistic assets.
6. practice multimodal writing using digital tools genres. (NCTE, 2018; ILA, 2020)

Even with these recommendations and as the practice of writing has become increasingly digital and multimodal, writing assessment demands in secondary schools have made the teaching of writing more constrained by placing ever greater emphasis on highly scripted writing forms.

For example, since the implementation of the Common Core State Standards, there has been great attention to teaching argumentative and persuasive writing. As a result, other kinds of writing—including narrative, poetic, or creative writing—have been all but eliminated from the curriculum. Teachers of writing continue to teach formulaic formats like the five-paragraph essay, constructed response (short essay answers to standards-based comprehension questions on timed tests), and varying forms of highly structured argument. These practices are prompted by a pervasive belief that argumentative and persuasive writing is, somehow, more serious than other kinds and that these are the modes that count in college and academic writing. Although assigning mostly argumentative and persuasive writing may fit our best intentions in preparing students to pass high-stakes exams, these two modes in no way represent the diverse array of written genres produced in the world. Nor do they encourage students to draw from their diverse lived experiences to communicate their ideas for audiences and purposes beyond the school walls.

This book offers a rigorous and timely approach to teaching writing, using genre as a framework that is intended to help students see how writing is tied to social purposes, contexts, and expectations. The genre framework offers an inclusive and expansive approach that allows students to bring their whole selves to the page while engaging in a series of scholarly moves: sharing and making sense of new ideas and information, defining what they care about and why, and engaging with real audiences for purposes that matter to them deeply. The genre approach also allows teachers of writing to move beyond narrow definitions of what counts as writing, and to support students' diverse learning styles and interests.

The Organization of this Book

This book's alternative framework for designing and implementing a secondary writing curriculum places a central emphasis on helping students gain the experience they need to write with confidence in academic and civic life. Each chapter offers approaches to teaching a specific genre. These are not genres from days of old. The genres curated in these pages are current, often multimodal writing used across disciplines to make sense of thoughts and lived experience, to communicate ideas, and to impact positive social change. These are genres that speak to students who are already immersed in rich and multifaceted literacy practices through social media, gaming, and new technologies. Many of these genres require research and close reading while also allowing students to tap into their interests and lived experiences. My hope is that these genres will also appeal to teachers of writing who want to expand their curriculum in innovative and exciting ways.

In the chapters that follow, we will explore eight different genres that were chosen with an eye toward writing for civic and academic engagement. This book is about harnessing the energy, curiosity, lived experience, interest, and potential of our students. It invites the teaching of different genres for real purposes, audiences, and initiatives in mind. It also invites writers to engage with multimodal literacies through every aspect of invention, research, revision, and reflection.

Chapter 1 discusses the **turning point essay**: a genre focused on an experience or event in the writer's life that profoundly impacts who they are or what they care about. Turning point essays may also lend themselves to some commonly taught subgenres such as college admission or scholarship application essays. This essay is an opportunity to describe a pivotal point in the writer's life when they learned something important in relation to who they want to be or how they hope to participate or act in the world. It offers a wonderful way to have students share experiences from their lives that have shaped who they are and what they care about. The turning point essay is a genre to use early in a semester or school year to get to know your students and to have them build community and a safe space in the writing classroom.

Chapter 2 shares the teaching of the **artist statement**: a written introduction to a creative work that provides insight or background to contextualize a creative piece. The artist statement is an example of an ever-evolving genre used by professional artists to help readers or viewers of their work interpret or make sense of it in public or private spaces such as museums, libraries, community centers, and even airports. Artist statements are simple and direct pieces that share the artist's vision without telling the reader how to feel about or react to their creative work. Teachers may use this short genre as a pairing with other creative projects (e.g., a painting, poem, collage, or digital story) in response to literature or reading.

Chapter 3 is about the **public service announcement** or PSA: a form of multimodal communication that tries to persuade the audience to act or make a change. A PSA is like an advertisement, but generally urges a desired action or behavior rather than a purchase. They are often created to promote programs sponsored by nonprofit organizations or by federal, state, and local governments. A PSA is typically brief in written content, as the intention is to quickly inform and persuade the audience using easily absorbed data or facts. It often uses a combination of visual and textual written forms to make a compelling argument. PSAs may be written as stand-alone assignments or in connection to reading about current events or nonfiction texts.

Chapter 4 offers an instructional approach to teaching the **infographic**: the now ubiquitous genre that presents information visually in an easy-to-read format. Infographics typically combine words and images or graphic organizers to quickly give an overview of a topic or set of information such as findings related to a specific aspect of research or the steps of a process. Infographics give students hands-on experience considering and utilizing visual design to represent information clearly and effectively. The infographic also can act as a bridge to help students move past formulaic writing. Its organizational structure features clear, visual segments between components of the content, which provide a familiar kind of structure or parameter to work within. This can serve as a bridge between what they are used to in structure and boundaries with writing while also new freedom to present their ideas and information using visual design and research. Assigning an infographic provides an opportunity for students to recognize the intentionality and strategy at work in a rhetorical situation. They must consider their audience and purpose and draw on their own expertise as they negotiate the parameters of a new genre.

Chapter 5 shares an approach to teaching a genre known as the **op-ed** (short for "opposite the editorial page"): typically letters or essays to the editor, written to express an opinion that doesn't necessarily align with that expressed by the publication in which it appears. Crafting an op-ed piece challenges the writer to think in new or unique ways about a topic of interest and engage with up-to-date research to make an argument that is convincing. Students may write about current events, community issues, or ideas that they care about deeply. They may write for the school paper, community newsletters or papers, or online blogs or news sources. This genre is a wonderful tool for students to experience how writing gives them agency and access in their communities and beyond.

Chapter 6 describes the teaching of a **profile essay**: the story of a unique individual. This genre offers an opportunity for the writer to interview a person in their lives with a shared passion or someone in a career or life pathway the writer is interested in exploring. The profile essay is a narrative genre that focuses on an individual to tell their story and to highlight their contributions, life choices, and wisdom or expertise. Profile essays are often featured in magazines or news venues, often as a part of a sports or arts broadcast. These are in-depth stories of individuals' lives or careers and offer the writer a lens into another person's perspective and experience. The profile essay requires the writer to draw from primary and secondary research to carefully craft the story of an individual in their community.

Chapter 7 focuses on the teaching of the **podcast**: a digital audio episode about a specific topic. Podcasts offer a timely way to engage students in multimodal writing. The podcast can be assigned as an individual or group project and involves scriptwriting, voice-over recording and the blending of music or sounds. To create a podcast, writers must research information on a topic they feel connected to and can discuss with relative ease, represent a range of viewpoints, and provide context and commentary for the listener. Podcasts are used to tell stories, to share information, and to make arguments to influence others. To figure out their format and approach to this genre writers must first identify their audience and purpose.

The final chapter, Chapter 8, offers an invitation to teach the **proposal**: a genre used in college, the workplace, and the community to suggest and communicate a plan for a specific audience and purpose. The plan could be for almost anything: a book to be written, a community space to be built, a club to be formed, and so on. Writers create proposals to apply for grants and fellowships, to obtain permission to change their neighborhoods (e.g., by adding a mural, a community garden, or a speed bump), to suggest a partnership or start up a small business, and even to recommend new legislation. Proposal writing gives students a chance to think outside the box about how to describe their vision for a positive change and to outline the steps needed to effect it.

After a general introduction to the featured genre, each chapter is organized into the following sections:

- *Assignment Details*: suggestions for structuring a genre-based writing
  assignment
- *Reading Connection*: ways to connect students' writing in that genre with
  their reading
- *Writing Workshop Tips*: ideas for incorporating the genre into a writing
  workshop during mini lessons, writing, or sharing time
- *Digital Tools*: recommendations for using easily available tools and apps
  that students can access on phones or computers to incorporate images,
  sound, photos, etc.
- *Extensions or Adaptations of the Assignment*: additional ways to extend the
  assignment or tailor it to your students' needs and interests
- *Suggested Model Texts*: a list of recommended texts students can read to
  get a sense of the genre
- *Sample Assignment*: one example of how a genre-focused assignment
  might be structured
- *Examples of Student Writing*: two completed assignments in each genre
  from students in middle or high school or the first year of college

What I'm calling the framework for the genre approach to teaching writing
is presented in the first five sections listed above, focused on the structure,
content, and delivery of lessons. At the end of each chapter are a few additional resources to help with planning your assignments: lists of published
model texts, a sample assignment I've used with my students, and samples
of student writing in that genre to use as peer mentor texts.

The mentor texts in these chapters are intended to support teachers
interested in expanding their writing curriculum to include a wide range of
innovative genres that work alongside the teaching of literature, literature
circles, and book choice. Each chapter provides sample model texts to share
with students to introduce each genre. I believe every new writing unit or
assignment should begin with reading and that the teaching of reading and
writing should be intertwined. Each chapter of this book focuses on a specific
genre, and I provide examples of model texts that may be used as a teaching
tool to show students the way each genre works for a variety of audiences

and purposes. The goal is to have students practice reading as writers and to look for the common features and repeated patterns that make up a genre so they can then do so on their own. Reading model texts gives our students the opportunity to recognize the way genres work and how and why they are used in the world. It also gives students an opportunity to read closely and carefully, to annotate and make sense of the moves writers make and why.

Students often struggle with writing, not because of a lack of ability or skill, but because they don't understand the writing assignment. Even with the very best of intentions, we too often set our students up to struggle by giving them writing assignments with vague instructions and unclear purposes. Or we give our students overly scripted and formulaic writing assignments that do not allow them to invest in or care about the topic or to understand the wider purpose or audience beyond the teacher or classroom. Thus, I provide sample writing assignments for each genre that you may use with your students or adapt as desired to fit your context and curriculum. These assignments include some of the main genre elements for each genre, with the understanding that if students learn these elements and include them, they will have a chance to create a successful product. I use these elements to guide students toward the expected outcome but also to plan the mini lesson and instruction I provide within the unit. My ethos in the teaching of any genre is that if I am going to require specific genre elements, then I need to teach students what they are and how to use them, give them examples (these are found in the model texts), and give them time to practice. Each sample assignment in the chapters that follow provides students with an understanding of the task at hand, the audience and purpose, and four to five key genre elements to include to create the genre. None of these assignments are meant as a formula to follow, but as invitations and guides for you and your students.

Finally, each chapter also provides samples of student writing for the genre of focus. The writing samples are meant for you to use as model texts alongside the professionally published mentor texts. Thus, your students may see how other adolescent writers have taken up the writing invitations and written from their own lens based on their unique interests, experiences, and contexts. Many of the included student samples are from the first-year college students I work with as part of an Early Start program I lead, which is a bridge program from high school to college and takes place two weeks before the fall semester at my university. These students are just weeks out of their high school classrooms. I invite them to write many of the genres included in this book as they begin their journey as college writers. I also include student writing examples from sixth- through 12th-grade students from many of the English Language Arts classrooms of amazing teachers I work with in my writing project site and in my English Education program who use this genre approach to teaching writing. Along with student examples, I also include examples of writing from teachers to demonstrate the genres and to make visible the work of teachers as writers. One of the core beliefs of the National Writing Project, a site of knowledge and research production for the teaching of writing and the oldest professional development network for teachers of writing, is that we as teachers of writing may benefit our students by showing our own writing process and products. By sharing our writing, we create a lens into the adult world through story, topic, and writing process. We also can share our strategies and process for writing these genres alongside our students and demystify the writing process by revealing our own trials and success. We can test out what works and what doesn't in our own writing and bring this in to show students. The teacher examples provided in these chapters are written by teachers in my writing project who created these for their students and to send out for publication, thus opening the walls of their classrooms. The teacher writing samples serve as models to use with students alongside the student and professional examples or as an invitation for you to write your own model to share with your students.

We want our students to understand and experience how writing is a tool they can take with them anywhere to voice their ideas, to make sense of their lived experience, to accomplish personal and professional goals and required tasks, and to act or make change in their lives and in the lives of others. While I offer invitations to teach specific genres in this book, I believe the framework in this book can be applied to other genres as well and adapted for use in multiple contexts for diverse student populations. My intention is that you will take up the ideas in this book and change or expand them to fit your school contexts and the needs of your students.

Above all, this book is an invitation to secondary teachers of writing—who are faced with increased and ever-shifting pressures to demonstrate student success on high-stakes tests—to allow themselves some choice in their writing curriculum, and to give their students the freedom to explore topics and formats about which they are passionate. May the reading of *Next Generation Genres* refresh your view of writing as a vital tool for all students to navigate different audiences, prepare for their future lives, and influence the world around them for the better—all while finding their own voices.

References

International Literacy Association. (2020). Research advisory: Teaching writing to improve reading skills. Retrieved February 17, 2022, from: https://www.literacyworldwide.org/docs/default-source/where-we-stand/ila-teaching-writing-to-improve-reading-skills.pdf

Martin, P. P. (1996). *El milagro and other stories*. Tucson, Arizona: University of Arizona Press.

National Council for Teachers of English. (2018). *Understanding the teaching of writing: Guiding principles*. Retrieved February 17, 2022, from https://ncte.org/statement/teachingcomposition/

NEXT
GENERATION
GENRES

CHAPTER 1

The Turning Point Narrative

By the time our students enter our classrooms, they have already experienced profound events in their lives that have shaped who they are and what they care about. These events may be as big or small as a gift, a move, a divorce, a death, an award, a change in friendship, an illness, or an observation. I think of these moments or life events as turning points. They are shifts in awareness or understanding of an issue, topic, or cause. Our students navigate the complexity of life and the decisions of adults in their lives constantly, and a writing classroom is a place where we can give them a chance to reflect on and make sense of their lived experience of turning points. If we don't write and reflect about these events in our lives, we run the risk of never taking hold of what matters to us most deeply and making decisions and choices about our life pathways that are not necessarily our own.

This chapter focuses on teaching a turning point narrative, a narrative essay describing a turning point in an individual's life when they learned something important about who they want to be, what they value, or how they hope to participate or act in the world. I have taught this essay from sixth grade through college, and no matter the age or grade level, students come to this invitation with powerful stories of turning points that have shaped their young lives. I most recently taught this essay in a two-week college bridge program for incoming first-year students at my university. Although I currently use this assignment with entering college students, it is an ideal fit for secondary students of all grade levels. It is an excellent essay to use at the beginning of the school year: It allows students to share a little about themselves, helps teachers get to know their students, and enables students to write about something they know and care about deeply.

As a high school English teacher, I often framed the curriculum around issues of activism and changemaking. In preparing this curriculum, I read autobiographies, biographies, and memoirs about activists worldwide (Early Singer, 2006). Through this reading, I noticed that people are committed to making positive changes in each life pathway. They often experience turning points in their lives that influence who or what they care about and propel them into working toward change. For example, in her recent memoir, *The Moment of Lift* (2019), Melinda Gates describes her travels to rural and poor villages throughout the world to help provide better access to health care and contraception. However, as she traveled and listened to women tell their stories, she realized she needed to broaden her focus to support women's rights of all kinds. For Gates, the act of listening to women's voices and genuinely taking the time to hear their stories to learn who they were and what they needed to be healthy served as a turning point in her work as an activist. She realized she needed to consider and take up women's rights more generally if she was to help lift them out of poverty; focus on contraception was not enough.

The turning point narrative is an essay that examines a point in our lives that changed us in ways from which we can move forward. A turning point may happen when we shift perspective to incorporate new ideas or ways of seeing, like Gates supporting women's rights. Or it may be an experience when we are stopped in our tracks and moved deeply, or when we have a sense of profound clarity or appreciation, or when we are hurt or let down. When my students complete turning point essays, they often write about the death of a loved one, the birth of a sibling, a move, the death of a dog, a failing grade, a divorce—if this created a turning point. The important aspect of topic selection is if the student grew from the experience in some way: learned a lesson, realized something, or saw the issue in a new way. The experience does not have to be traumatic, but it can be. It should be an experience that students feel safe to share with others.

Assignment Details

Turning point writing emphasizes the importance of believing in what is possible when students write to tap into and share their own experiences to consider who they are, what they care about, and who they want to be in their current and future lives. Typically, the turning point essay is relatively brief (two to three pages), and you may want students to include visual images or use digital tools to accompany their essays (see Sample Turning Point Essay Assignment). Or they can write the essay and then create a short film with a voice-over to visually tell the story using digital tools such as iMovie. The piece centers on a time when the writer experienced a new understanding, a shift in perspective, or a deep investment in a particular topic. The main genre elements in the essay include: (1) a strong leading sentence that hooks the reader, (2) detailed description and narration, (3) reflection about the event, and (4) lessons learned. This invitation employs a broad definition of narrative writing, including analog or digital and visual texts (see Turning Point Essay Assignment).

Reading Connection

The writing of turning point essays may be nicely paired with the literature you already use in your English language arts curriculum. Before teaching the turning point narrative, you may invite students to connect to the book or essays they have read or think about the books and the characters' stories they will read over the year. In almost every book, whether fiction or nonfiction, a character or characters experience a turning point that profoundly shifts the course of their lives. Students can examine the different turning points characters face throughout a unit, a semester, or a year. This is a way to create a link between texts and to find commonalities across human experience.

Along with using turning points as an overarching theme for reading, you may also select a variety of texts before introducing turning point essays to serve as models for students in writing their own essays. Offering a variety of essays, video clips, and even music to highlight turning points (see Model Texts) gives students a sense of different ways writers create and share narratives about pivotal events. For example, I often use an essay written by John McPhee in *Sierra Magazine* (2010) titled "Swimming with Canoes" as an example of a turning point narrative. He describes the repetitive and careful study of learning to canoe each summer as a child at a summer camp in Maine. Toward the end of the piece, McPhee shares a memory of an accident that took place as he paddled with a friend into a gorge when they hit rough water, and their canoe tipped over. McPhee's leg was caught, and he could not get out of the boat. He describes the moment of falling underwater and realizing he was stuck. "I struggled to get the foot free, but it wouldn't come. Upside down in billows of water, I could not get out" (p. 34). He recognizes, in retrospect, that this was a moment when ordinarily he would have panicked. Instead, his persistent practice canoeing granted him the ability to act in a situation to save his own life, which he hadn't realized he had been preparing for all along. This essay relays this memory as a turning point in McPhee's young life when he both learned his capability and strength and benefited from his hard work and practice. This piece is so powerful because, like McPhee, we all have events that change our ways of understanding the world and recognizing our place and strength within it. These moments may not be life or death, like McPhee's, but they are equally life changing.

I use Gloria Anzaldúa's (1987) essay, "How to Train a Wild Tongue," which begins with a powerful description of a dentist working in her mouth to clean out roots to put a cap on a tooth and yelling at her that they "are going to have to control your tongue." The lead in this essay describes the memory of the dentist telling her to control her wild tongue, which resonates as a metaphor for other kinds of borders and silencing Anzaldúa experienced and witnessed in her life growing up as a Chicana migrant worker. She uses her personal experience and memory of being silenced to make an argument against linguistic and cultural oppression, which has become the focus of her life's work as a leading Chicana feminist scholar.

Another turning point piece I give students opportunities to read in preparation for writing their own is the opening chapter of Richard Rodriguez's autobiography, *Hunger of Memory* (1983). In this chapter, Rodriguez describes entering a private Catholic school as a child knowing only fifty words of English. He was the only native Spanish speaker in a class of white English speakers. He uses his memory of entering and adapting to an English-only school to share what shapes his lens as a Mexican-

American writer and scholar vehemently opposed to bilingual education programs.

The above two examples show how writers may narrate a turning point in their lives to make an argument about a significant issue they care about deeply. It helps students understand how the stories from their lives can relate to broader issues they care about and how these personal stories are often the reason they feel invested in specific topics.

Sharing model texts of different turning point pieces is an effective way for students to start to gain familiarity with this genre. Jason Reynolds's "Eleven Minutes: A Call from Kobe Bryant" describes a turning point Reynolds experienced upon hearing the news that his childhood hero, Kobe Bryant, had died tragically in a helicopter crash. When Reynolds heard this news, his mind flashed back to the memory of an unexpected phone call he had received from Bryant years before. The turning point for Reynolds was now, with the news of this loss of a hero, understanding that the call meant something more profound in his life than he had understood at the time:

> *But in the wake of his death, one of the many things I can't stop thinking about is that call. That moment I answered the phone, and the ease in which he said, "How you doing?" The familiarity of it all. Perhaps it was because he knew more than anyone that he was Kobe Bryant, a giant, an icon, a hero to so many. But I can't help but think it was something else. Something less performative. That just like my mother talks to me like a mother talks to a son—like family talks to family—to keep me grounded, I wonder if Kobe simply understood that as much as he was the Black Mamba on the court, basketball, like life, doesn't work properly unless it touches the ground, over and over again.* (2020)

This turning point example describes how Reynolds came to see the 11-minute exchange with Bryant as a moment of connection, regardless of fame.

I often use Matt de la Peña's short story, "How to Transform an Everyday, Ordinary Hoop Course into a Place of Higher Learning and You at the Podium" from the *Flying Lessons* collection (Oh, 2017) as an example of a turning point narrative. This piece is rich with a discussion about a turning point in de la Peña's life. We closely analyze the rhetorical choices de la Peña uses in the first few pages, the turning point, the climax, and his play off the traditional and overused "what I did last summer" essay. De la Peña extends time through thick descriptions, and he makes us sit in his experience and see, hear, and feel what he does. As a class, we discuss his sentence variety, commas, dashes, and use of vivid verbs, descriptions, and dialogue. Students closely read the paragraphs in the first pages of this story and the end of the piece, where the turning point happens. This way, they luxuriate in their reading and pull out as many of the moves the writer makes to share his memory and meaning. Students love to point out the way de la Peña plays with sentence variety and uses an accordion-like structure by which long sentences are connected and mixed with concise ones. We workshop this, share what we find with partners or in small groups, and then use what clicks as strategies to take up in our essays. No matter the texts you share with students as examples of turning points, the idea is to help them think about how experiences can change us in powerful ways and how these experiences can shape us with reflection and understanding.

You can offer guiding questions to support the close reading of the model texts to help students think about the author's choices. Possible guiding questions include:

- Does the writer use foreshadowing to hint at what may be the turning point?
- Where does the turning point happen in the text? Why does it occur there?
- What writing choices does the author make at the turning point?
- Are the choices the same or different from the text surrounding them?
- How does the turning point change the writer?
- Is there a change in belief, value, perspective, or understanding?
- How do you think the writer wants the reader to react to this turning point and change?
- How do you react to this turning point and change?
- What may be the universal lesson or understanding that emerges from the text?

Writing Workshop Tip:
Mini Lesson Ideas for Invention and Brainstorming

What writers need at any grade level are time and support getting started in writing all genres. You can turn to two strategies repeatedly to give students ways into their writing that feel less daunting than a blank page: lists and doodle mapping.

Lists

To help students begin from a place of abundance in their writing the turning point narrative, I ask students to take 2–3 minutes to create a list of memories of turning points in their lives. Multiple lists are excellent and can be generative in prewriting, and it's also okay if students have one concise list. Sometimes students know what they want to write about from the get-go. Others need help generating ideas and feeling comfortable with expanding on the assignment.

Student topics can be about trips to see grandparents, camping, scouting, moving, an illness, loss (death of a pet or loved one), sporting events, fandom, gaming, and music. One year, one of my seniors wrote about the first time she ever ate blue cheese and how this event sparked her passion and interest in cheese. Since that tasty moment, she has become a cheese connoisseur and hopes one day to travel to Paris to visit cheese shops and perhaps open her own cheese shop eventually. One of my first-year college students wrote about her experience as an African American young woman trying to figure out her identity in connection to language. She had always felt like an imposter because of the way she speaks and felt she was caught between two worlds because of her skin color and language use. She used the turning point essay as an opportunity to share how a TED Talk changed her perspective about how she perceives herself. This led her to stop battling with others to help them see her and instead to become comfortable in how she sees herself (see Turning Point Student Example 2 for full essay).

Doodle Mapping

One quick strategy to help students flesh out their topic choice is to create a doodle map of their turning point memory. A doodle map combines quick drawings, annotations, and notes to capture a memory or topic. Students usually have no problem doodling pieces of their memory, and I offer a few questions to help them write alongside their images:

- How would I narrate this memory? Share your best description of what you remember.
- How would someone else narrate this memory? Consider a witness, bystander, or passerby looking in on this experience.
- Answer the question: "So what?" Why does this experience matter to me?
- Why might this experience matter to my audience?
- What new insight might my audience gain from reading about my turning point?

This exercise in writing from differing perspectives gives students agency to think about memory and experience from diverse lenses and to make the experience clear for others while still claiming the memory as their own. It also helps students stop and start the turning point narrative without worrying about a beginning, middle, or end and with no stakes attached. In a reflection about this kind of prewriting, one of my students wrote, "Warm-up writing can help from feeling stiff and not knowing what to put on the page."

One of my students, Margarita, wrote about her reaction to a children's movie, *Zooptopia*. In her answer to the first question in this exercise, "How would I narrate this memory?" she dives into her memory of watching the movie for the first time and having an unexpected and strong reaction to the story:

> *A few years ago, I saw* Zootopia *for the first time. For a kid's movie, it touches well on the idea of prejudice and racial profiling. With all that considered, I ended up sobbing at a flashback scene where the fox as a child is bullied and told that predators and prey could never be friends. To this day, I can't talk about that scene without feeling a heaviness in my heart. Why though? Because for me, it wasn't just a fox, it wasn't just a movie, it was a kid somewhere out there in real life who is being bullied, and there was nothing I could do about it.*

Margarita describes how she experienced bullying from her friends in high school and had years of feeling lonely and isolated. Somehow, watching this movie allowed her to reflect and identify with characters, even if they were animated on a screen. This reminded her of her past. At the end of her essay, she describes her rediscovered understanding about her future self. When she answered the question, "So what?" about this memory, she wrote the following:

> *It took me an entire year of being alone, having no friends, and coaching gymnastics constantly to realize that I'm okay with being alone, that it's okay to be alone and find value and self-worth in myself. I'm not dramatic; I'm empathic. And that's okay, that's what makes me different from a dolphin and Jeffrey Dahmer. The only difference now is that there's no way to have good mental health and make everyone's problems your own. I can't. I wish I could. What I can do is care about the truly important things to me. This moment has shown me how powerful it is to be comfortable with yourself; I've decided to major in something that I'm passionate about and see myself happy in the long run.*

Although Margarita wrote the above paragraph in this early warm-up exercise to get started with the turning point essay, she ended up using it as part of her conclusion for her piece in the final draft because it explains the larger message of the essay. It's helpful to explain to students how answering this question (the "So what?" or universal theme) is a way of moving outward as a writer in a narrative, so the piece is not only turning inward to recall the personal experience. The universal theme is a turn the writer makes in the narrative to relay why the experience matters to the writer and how it connects to a more significant issue in human experience.

Digital Tools

You may have students incorporate digital media into the production of the turning point narrative. The media may be in a digital story using a voice-over of the written narrative with digital images, song, film, and so on. It's helpful to provide several examples of media tools or sources for students in creating digital components or platforms for sharing their narratives. Students can write their narratives and then present them using digital storytelling. Or they can read their pieces aloud and share in person or using FlipGrid or VoiceThread. Other students create videos using Adobe Spark or Canva or record a podcast with Audacity or GarageBand. You can even have students create a digital book as a class using BookCreator or Storybird. The possibilities are endless and ever evolving. The more we invite students to take advantage of these tools and tap into the tools they already use in their lives, the more we can add layers to telling their stories and relevance for writing in the digital age.

Students also love using photographs from their phones to illustrate their narratives. One of my first-year college students wrote her turning point narrative about frequent trips to Arizona as a young girl to visit her grandparents. She described her turning points as a series of events when her grandfather took her to visit the Arizona State University campus. She begins her piece, "ASU has been the plan for me since I was in the womb. Growing up, my family would take many weekend trips to Phoenix to attend ASU football games and tailgate parties with loads of our extended family and friends. I grew up knowing this was the school I was meant to go to." Throughout her essay, Bella includes photographs of her with her grandparents on these college visits wearing ASU clothing, pictures of her grandfather in the military, a photo of her graduating high school, and a picture of her on her first day of college. These images help tell her story and create a feeling of intimacy with the reader. (See Student Essay Example 2 for full essay; also see the Author's Note concerning privacy and subject permission.)

Extensions

Biography-driven writing calls on many, if not all, of the same kinds of skills used in various forms of academic writing. For example, in biography-driven writing, students must draw from research, use rhetorical devices (e.g., logos, pathos, and ethos), synthesize ideas, and maintain awareness of audience and purpose. These personal and experience-based writing forms also often use the first person. Students need to understand that academia does not only exist in the third person. College writers navigate and employ different rhetorical approaches, voices, and strategies depending on the genre they are working on.

Along with the turning point essay workshop, you may incorporate a variety of biography-driven genres into your curriculum. For example, at the beginning of the semester, I often teach a writing workshop using the "My Name" chapter vignette from Sandra Cisneros's *House on Mango Street* (1991) and a selection of children's books about naming (Choi, 2003; Recorvits and Swiatkowska, 2014; Martinez-Neal, 2018). I ask students to write their name vignettes and research family stories and linguistic meanings behind their names. I also invite students to write literacy narratives and share how they have gained or witnessed literacy throughout their lives.

The turning point essay can also be used as the start for writing college admission or scholarship essays. High school students typically write college admission essays during their junior year or the first semester of their senior year as part of the college application process. For many colleges and universities, the admission essay is the only opportunity to learn about applicants personally, and for many students, this genre can feel intimidating and hard to start. Giving students opportunities to write and reflect on pivotal experiences in their lives, like the turning point essay, allows them to bring in and share their lived experiences within the work we do in school. It also allows them to make sense of the experience for a larger audience beyond themselves and their teacher. You may find ways of having students share their turning point essays in a final reading in class, online using Flipgrid or VoiceThread, or in a silent read-around where students move around the classroom to read one another's writing and comment on it in a gallery-like arrangement. This kind of writing and sharing builds community and shows students' unique and powerful lives and interests within a learning community. As one of my students reflected in a note to me after reading the turning point essays of her classmates, "It's been so interesting reading other people's turning points. It has made me realize how different we all are and how all of our stories tell the story of who we are in this room together in a way I would never have realized without the writing."

TURNING POINT MODEL TEXTS

Essays and Book Chapters

Alexie, S. (2011). Superman and me. In S. Cohen. (Ed.), *50 Essays: A portable anthology* (3rd ed., pp. 15–19). Bedford.

Anzaldúa, G. (1987). How to tame a wild tongue. In *Borderlands/La frontera: The new mestiza* (pp. 53–64). Aunt Lute Books.

de la Peña, M. (2018). How to transform an everyday, ordinary hoop court into a place of higher learning and you at the podium. In E. Oh (Ed.), *Flying Lessons & Other Stories* (pp. 1–22). Yearling.

McPhee, J. (1998, August 2). Swimming with canoes. *The New Yorker* (pp. 33–34).

Orwell, G. (1936). Shooting an elephant. *New Writing* (2). https://www.orwell foundation.com/the-orwell-foundation/orwell/essays-and-other-works/shooting-an-elephant/

X, Malcolm. (2011). Learning to read. In S. Cohen. (Ed.), *50 Essays: A portable anthology* (3rd ed., pp. 257–266). Bedford.

Zauner, M. (2018, August 20). Crying in H Mart. *The New Yorker*. https://www.newyorker.com/culture/culture-desk/crying-in-h-mart

YA Literature

Wonder by R. J. Palacio (Knopf, 2012). This is a popular text in the younger middle grades. I'm thinking of how it opens with a turning point as the main character attends public school for the first time. He was homeschooled previously due to his facial disfigurement. We get the description of his fears, anxieties, and courage across that turning point.

Persepolis: The Story of a Childhood by Marjane Satrapi (Pantheon, 2004). This is a historical graphic novel based on the author's life. It opens with a rapid sequence of life before and after the 1979 Islamic Revolution in Iran. It is excellent for middle grades and shows (and tells) very powerfully the radical government's effect on the lives of the people, girls and women especially. Great voice and storytelling.

Now Is the Time for Running by Michael Williams (Little, Brown, 2011). Historical fiction whose opening chapters (1–4) detail life in a small village in Zimbabwe before and after a massacre by a local military warlord.

CONTINUED

Heart-wrenching, fast-paced, gripping. A good example of details and storytelling to capture the readers' hearts.

Revolution by Deborah Wiles (Scholastic, 2013). Historical fiction that blends modes with historical imagery and quotes. While a longer book, the first few chapters detail the summer before and when civil rights groups flood Mississippi as the freedom summer. The main character is a kid who sneaks into a (Whites-only) pool at night, only to find an African American boy swimming there. The turning point happens as the kid realizes that the African American boy should be equal.

Podcast

Kumanyika, Chenjerai. (1997, March 28). "The two times I met Laurence Fishburne." The Moth. https://themoth.org/stories/the-two-times-i-met -laurence-fishburne

Twitter

Teju Cole's Twitter essay on immigration, "A Piece of the Wall" (March 13, 2014), could have been published in a more traditional avenue (like *The Atlantic*, where he has published before); he chose Twitter for its format and reach (twitter.com/tejucole/timelines/444262126954110977?lang=en).

Music

Look up and consider the lyrics of a favorite song about a turning point: One example (shot on an iPhone) is Selena Gomez's *Lose You to Love Me* (but see the Author's Note on copyright in general and song lyrics in particular; https://www.youtube.com/watch?v=zlJDTxahav0).

TURNING POINT ESSAY SAMPLE ASSIGNMENT

Purpose: This essay is based on the premise that understanding your approach to writing in college and the humanities is fundamentally connected to your own experience, interests, investment, and insight as a person. You will use writing and artifacts to tell the story of where you come from, how you come from connects to who you are, and what you hope to study and pursue in your future pathways as a college student and person. This essay will focus on a turning point in your life that led you to care about, become invested in, or want to study and work on a specific issue, topic, or cause. As such, you will write a brief (400–750 word) turning point narrative in which you explore the roots of your interest in or thinking about a particular issue that matters to you deeply and the way this turning point may shape your ways of thinking about your college studies and life. This piece will be accompanied by five artifacts (digital or crafted) to help tell your story.

Genre: This is a narrative essay. It should be in the first person. It is about YOU. It tells your story of a turning point in your life. Your experience and ability to tap into, reflect on, and think about your own lived experience and how it influences your goals and decisions are crucial in becoming and being a successful college student.

Audience: Your peers and ME

Length: 400–750 amazing words! It can be longer, but not much!

Sources: Use a quote from an article, a song lyric, and line of poetry, or any outside source that helps you tell your story well. This quote may begin your piece or be a part of it. It should NOT be plopped in. Please cite your source(s) using MLA or APA format.

Artifacts: This piece will be accompanied by five artifacts (digital or crafted) to help tell your story.

These may be copied photographs, collages, paintings, maps, or postcards (see Author's Note on copyright). It's up to you! Each artifact needs to be accompanied by a brief description or annotation to explain it.

Format: Times New Roman, 12pt font, double spaced, spell-checked, and with a great title.

First-Year College Student

My Tata's Story

ASU has been the plan for me since I was in the womb. Growing up, my family would take many weekend trips to Phoenix to attend ASU football games and tailgate parties with loads of our extended family and friends. I grew up knowing this was the school I was meant to go to. I never considered other schools. I never knew the story of why so many of my relatives before me also came on this journey and stepped foot onto this campus. What I did know was that it was up to me to get here and follow roughly similar paths as my family members.

As I got older, our family trips to ASU became less frequent as my Tata's (Grandfather) medical issues increased. I had never realized that those trips to the campus were made possible because of him and were mainly for him. When I was around fourteen or fifteen, I visited my Nina (Godmother) for a weekend in Phoenix. I am from Bisbee, Arizona, and Phoenix is at least 3 hours away by car, depending on traffic. One day we were folding some of my Nina's clothes and I was babbling about how much I loved Phoenix and big cities. I mentioned that I was going to go to ASU for college and she told me a story that everyone in my family seemed to know but me. I remember we were mating socks and my Nina finally started in: My Tata graduated from Bisbee High School (where I also graduated) and had been accepted into Arizona State University, Northern Arizona University, and the University of Arizona. Obviously, he chose ASU. He came from a poor Mexican family that lived up the canyon in Old Bisbee. He was the oldest of nine and he wasn't sure how he was going to pay for college or move away from family, but he did. He hitchhiked to Phoenix and made his way to ASU, where he attended for about two years.

Eventually he began getting overwhelmed socially, academically, and financially. He couldn't afford to live on campus, so he lived further off campus which lowered his motivation to coming to school while working multiple jobs. This also meant he had about three other roommates who were all older than he was, some seniors, some graduated and all slacking off; he soon started doing the same things. He wasn't just having fun; he was having too much fun and rarely going to class. He stopped doing his work and finally he just withdrew completely. He went back home to Bisbee where he soon was drafted to the Vietnam War. He left and served for a few years before getting honorably discharged. After this, many of my relatives started going to ASU and experiencing what he never got to. But, until hearing this story, I always thought my grandpa had graduated from ASU and started a family tradition of attending and graduating from this university. I didn't realize it was more complicated than that and that his love for this university and determination to see his family go to college was connected to his own story and to what he had hoped for himself but did not achieve.

I was shocked to hear he had dropped out. My Tata was the most intelligent person I knew. I could say an equation and he could solve it with no calculator. Hearing how he had to leave college totally freaked me out and made me doubt my own plan. If he couldn't make it, how could I? But despite that, I knew it was up to me to make this plan possible. I was his granddaughter, and none of his three girls made it to ASU no matter how much he silently pushed them to go to college. I knew I needed to do this for my Tata. So, my determination grew, and I tried harder and took more action to find out how I too could get into ASU. I was determined. As a junior in high school, I started going to college fairs with the seniors just to get as much information about ASU as I could. I started exploring all the possible majors and my options for ways to pay my tuition.

I remember when I found out I was accepted, I called my Tata immediately to tell him the news. He is hard of hearing, so when he answers the phone, you must wait about 10 seconds or so before speaking to give him time to put the phone on speaker. As soon as he said "Hello," I told him, "Tata guess what . . . I got into ASU." Right away he started cheering and telling me how proud of me he was, which meant and still means everything to me. I love the quote, "Time to open up a new chapter in life, and to explore a larger center" by Lillian Russe. These words represent my new beginning at ASU and a chance not only to explore a university and all it has to offer, but myself and my own strength and determination to grow and take opportunities as they come. Learning my grandfather's story of dropping out of college was a turning point in my life because it made me dig my heels in and decide that no matter what, I would go to the university of his dreams and graduate from it. I plan to have the best experiences I can and make my Tata proud.

TURNING POINT STUDENT EXAMPLE 2

First-Year College Student

Am I The Imposter?

When I was a junior in high school, I was assigned an English project to listen to and reflect on a TED Talk of my choice. While researching the topic, I stumbled upon a talk by Dena Simmons called "How Students of Color Confront Impostor Syndrome." When I read this title, I had no idea what racial imposter syndrome was, so I'm going to guess that you don't either. Racial imposter syndrome is the feeling of self-doubt when your internal racial identity doesn't match with others' perceptions of your racial identity. The social activist in me read this and fell in love. I instantly watched it and told everyone I knew about it.

Simmons talks about African American Vernacular English (AAVE) in the TED Talk. I was intrigued by this topic, so I decided to do some research into it. "Nonstandard Negro English" was a phrase created in the 1960s when the first large-scale modern linguistic studies of African American speech began. But in 1973, a group of African American scholars wanted to take the negative connotations away, so they renamed Nonstandard Negro English soon to be African American Vernacular English or AAVE. Some scholars contend that AAVE developed from the contact between speakers of West African languages and speakers of vernacular English varieties. According to such a view, West Africans learned English on plantations in the southern Coastal States. The dialect of the region influenced their learning of the language. African American Vernacular English is no shy creature in the classroom. AAVE creates a very sensitive barrier between the teacher and the student. This barrier can be like a language barrier in terms of the two parties understanding each other.

Going back to that TED Talk, Simmons explains her experience being a minority in a boarding school. "A teacher once instructed me in the hallway: "Aaaaaas-king." She said this loudly. "Dena, it's not 'axing,' like you're running around with an ax. That's silly." Now at this point, you can imagine the snickers of my classmates, but she continued: "Think about breaking the word into 'ass' and 'king,' and then put the two together to say it correctly—'Asking.'" This type of encounter is not uncommon for students of color to experience. I, myself, have had a similar experience. I always have, and still do, struggle with what I thought and wanted my racial identity to be. I wanted to make sure I reflected that loud enough that other people around me would also perceive that. My self-doubt set in, and I was stuck in this stage of "Oh my gosh, is that person just thinking that I'm acting/talking like a Black person?" I became good at this thing called the switch. Just like your everyday light switch, people of color switch the way they act around others in the same way. It becomes second nature, and you don't even realize you are doing it—everything from how you speak and walk to how you stand. Things you would never think about became so critical the older I became in my life. I grew up with white people telling me I talked so "proper" and Black people saying I talked "white." I was lost. I didn't know what side to believe.

Listening to this TED Talk and reflecting made me realize that how people perceive me will never change. I will always be the proper/white-speaking Black girl, and I had to be okay with that. I learned to be okay that people will perceive me differently than I want to be. And just this past year, I was working at my job, and I had gotten a phone call from a woman asking if we had a specific shirt in stock, and she wanted to come to pick it up. Well, when she came in, I checked her out. And while I was waiting for her receipt, she said, "You know when we were on the phone, I had no idea you were a Black girl." I looked at her and asked her why? She simply said, "Well, you don't talk . . . Black." Her sentence was slowly getting quieter since all my other coworkers at the time were Black. I simply smiled and handed her the receipt without a response and finally felt comfortable in my silence just being me.

References

Choi, Y. (2003). *The name jar.* Dragonfly Books

Gates, M. F., (2019). *The moment of lift: How empowering women changes the world.* New York, NY: Flatiron Books.

Early Singer, J. (2006). *Stirring up justice: Writing and reading to change the world.* Portsmouth, NH: Heinemann.

Marley, R. (2016). Quotes about travel and exploration. *Wander.* https://vocal .media/wander/quotes-about-travel-and-exploration.

Martinez-Neal, J. (2018). *Alma and how she got her name.* Candlewick Press.

Recorvits, H., & Swiatkowska, G. (2014). *My name is Yoon.* Square Fish Publisher.

TED. (November 2015). How students of color confront impostor syndrome/ Dina Simmons [video]. https://www.ted.com/talks/dena_simmons_ how_students_of_color_confront_impostor_syndrome?language=en

CHAPTER 2

The Artist Statement

My husband and my closest friend from college are both artists. This means that art and art shows have been a part of my life for over 25 years. I have enjoyed being a reader and editor of the artist statements of these two favorite people of mine, to help them prepare for art shows. I love how this genre works to share the artist's intention and creative process. Sometimes, the statement allows the artist to teach their audience history or content related to the piece. It makes the creative process as well as the artist's intent more transparent.

I first introduced the artist statement in my high school classroom as an example of this genre used out in the world. I shared my college friend's statements as real-world examples. I taught this genre as a way for students to share their thinking and process in connection to creative projects. For example, you can have students create self-portraits at the beginning of the year to share who they are and what they care about. Then, the artist statement is a perfect written genre to pair with visual portraits as a way for students to share their thinking, planning, and intentions behind their work. Another option is to have them choose a part of themselves to showcase (one that they are willing to share) and create a piece on that part of themselves. The artist statement lends itself to a sharing option that feels safe to students. I continue to teach the artist statement at the college level and with teachers in my writing project as well as with incoming students at the university. Here are two examples of artist statements teachers from my writing project wrote the first week of our summer institute to go along with their self-portrait of themselves as teachers. I invited all the teachers in the workshop to create self-portraits representing how they see themselves as teachers. This is a wonderful activity to do with secondary students in the beginning of a semester. You can have them create self-portraits without using photographs of themselves and then write artist statements to pair with the self-portraits. This first portrait was created with watercolor and represents the teacher's self, and the artist statement explains her thinking behind the painting.

FIGURE 2.1 **Self Portrait and Artist Statement Example 1**
ARTIST: Jessica, English Education Doctoral Student
MEDIUM: Watercolor Pencil

My Teacher Self

The first time I used watercolor pencils I was sitting on the back patio of my dorm room. In Jerusalem. Our school was located on Mount Scopus and our back patios looked out over the old city. The gold bowl atop the Dome of the Rock Mosque glimmered against a backdrop of colorful roofs and old, cobbled roads, surrounded by a large ancient wall. I liked the structure of the pencils but also the way that when a wet brush met each line, the strict strokes bled into something new. Something free. When painting something that is supposed to resemble me, the medium of the work should do that as well. I, too, like structure. I like lines that point me in the direction I should go and a detailed plan of how things should be done. I didn't change my major ten times like you are supposed to do in college. I decided on it when I was in seventh grade, and it never changed. But sometimes, everyone has to let go a little. The plan was to major in English Education as a practical back-up and then go on to law school. Up until my final semester of my undergrad, while studying for the LSAT, this remained my goal. Until I let my edges be touched by a wet brush that allowed the strokes to bleed in a way that hadn't been anticipated. I didn't go to law school. I ended up in the classroom teaching English. Just like a watercolor pencil—I want my students to know that things are never final. Sometimes, what we plan is not the way things should really be. A masterful sketch of colors can actually turn out so much better when we are willing to take some risks and let go.

In this next example, the teacher created a collage representing who she hopes to be as a teacher. She created an image with magazine clippings of an image representing her jumping off a diving board. Her artist statement explains her thinking behind the artwork:

FIGURE 2.2 Self Portrait and Artist Statement Example 2

ARTIST: Melissa, English Teacher

MEDIUM: Paper/Collage

Artist Statement

All the characters in the story of my teacher life are interchangeable. When I imagine who I want to be at my teacher best, I imagine myself as a diving board. To borrow terms from Alanis Morissette, I want to be a "platform from which [my students can] jump beyond themselves," to jump into something new and unfamiliar, to find their voices as they jump, to launch into themselves. So, in that sense, the woman jumping in this collage is each of my students, and their discoveries and mistakes and ah-ha's. The woman jumping is inviting others to take a similar leap. I am also the jumper, even on the bad days. My students have the power of a high dive. They hold me, scare me, and propel me.

I often have students create artist statements to accompany self-portraits at the beginning of the year or semester to share their representations of self and to build community. I also use artist statements to pair with culminating literature-based projects, such as scrapbooks and character portraits. Alternatively, to go alongside multigenre projects or portfolio collections of writing as a way for students to step back from the whole, reflect on their process, and share their major takeaways. I also have students write artist statements to accompany their multigenre character portfolios as a culminating project when they do a character study as we read a play. There are endless possibilities for ways to use this genre in your classroom.

The artist statement is a written introduction to a creative work that provides insight and background to contextualize the piece. This document can be used in multiple ways and can have various versions. Artist statements are used worldwide to communicate the meaning and process of artistic works in museums, libraries, and other public and private spaces. This genre is often a required part of proposal submission for artists when competing for grants, proposals for public and private works and artist residencies, and promotional materials (e.g., websites, pamphlets, and magazines).

The artist statement is an ever-evolving genre used by professional artists to help readers or viewers interpret and make sense of the artist's work. These statements are typically written in the first person and can be written as manifestos, lists, calls and submissions, public presentations, reflections, and descriptions. Most artist statements include a title, the date of production of the piece of art, the artist's name, materials used to create the piece, and a brief description or reflection on what the piece of art is meant to share, show, or teach.

Artist statements can be serious and take on an informative and formal tone or playful and informal one. The formality depends on the audience and purpose. The main objective is to share the artist's vision without telling the viewer/reader how to feel about or react to the creative work. It should directly relate to the art presented and work with the piece's message. Artist statements are simple, concise, clear, and direct. You want to encourage students to share the bare bones or meat of their creative endeavor and reflect on what they did for their project and why.

Reading Connection

When I introduce the artist statement in my classroom to accompany a creative project, I begin by giving students a diverse set of model texts so they can see the range of approaches to writing (see Artist Statement Model Texts). Then I let them have leeway in deciding how to approach theirs if they address the main genre expectations. An excellent way to have students see the diversity of this genre and how it is used in the world is to search for online art tours and the artist statements that accompany them. You can show students how to search by going to a museum website and simply doing an internal site search for "artist statement," and pieces with their statements will pop up. It helps students go to various creative spaces that may feel formal and far away, in addition to seeking out local galleries. For example, I ask students to search for artist statements from a significant metropolitan gallery, a mid-size city gallery, a small town or rural gallery, and a local (to them) art show or artist website. Also, whenever possible, I give students examples of artist statements written by teens so they see that this genre is not only for grown-ups or professional artists. A fantastic resource for artist statements written by youth can be found in Norton's (2022) *Coming of Age in 2020.*

Assignment Guide

The artist statement assignment follows the genre conventions of artist statements produced for a public showing of creative works. These are the genre elements I ask students to cover:

1. Title of creative work
2. Name of artist
3. Date of creative work
4. Artist process in creating the piece
5. Intention behind the piece
6. Creative materials

It is up to students' discretion to share this information in a formal paragraph, a list, a poem, a letter, or a creative form (see Artist Statement Assignment Example).

You may pair teaching the artist statement with a larger literacy project like a book study, creative endeavor, or multimodal writing form. The artist statement may be used as a reflection and assessment tool to support the reading of their creative work. It may be paired with the turning point narrative or the podcast in a gallery walk where students can move around a space, viewing, reading, and listening to the longer texts along with the artist statements in a gallery-like setting.

Writing Workshop Tip: Quick Writes as Drafting

A great way to get students to dive in and draft their artist statements is to do a series of quick writes with them where you ask them a question, have them write for two minutes and then stop, and then ask them another question. Asking students to write in these quick bursts to respond to a series of questions helps take away the stress of a blank page and gets them to think quickly with no attachment to a polished or finished piece. Here is the list of questions:

1. Who am I (name, age, grade)?
2. What was my creative practice for this project?
3. How was my work developed?
4. Why did I create it in this way?
5. What is the subject matter?
6. What was my intention or vision behind this piece?
7. What technique or materials did I use for the creative project (e.g., paint, magazines, digital images)?
8. What or who were my influences?
9. What story does this piece tell?

Once students have written a response to each of these questions (two minutes per question and no more), they start their artist statements to then go back into their quick start writing and add to, polish, and personalize.

Digital Tools

Students may utilize digital tools, images, or media to explain or share as part of their artist statements. Teachers may, for example, invite students to do a video talk as an artist statement using the audio record option on their phones or computers or using Flipgrid or VoiceThread. Alternatively, students may embed hyperlinks within digital artist statements that link to images, maps, or materials used in the creative process. You can have students present creative projects such as paintings, collages, photographs, heart maps, and poems in the classroom or school space in a gallery format. Their artist statements can be presented as QR codes for students to link to using tablets or phones. Depending on your school's policy toward student cell phone use, QR codes can be an excellent way to make writing and creative work come alive for students in this digital age. Students can use the free Audioboo app to record their artist statements. (Note: use the iPhone, not the iPad version of Audioboo; you cannot record using the iPad app.) With the Audioboo app, students can record a 3-minute audio file, add a photo if they want (this could be their creative work), a title, a QR code, and a button to publish the file to the web.

Extensions

It is always wonderful to take students to a museum to experience art and artist statements for themselves. If an art museum is out of the question because of logistics, often local libraries have art shows on display that are easy to visit, local, and free. This is also a great reason to partner with the art teacher at your school and have the art students create art statements for a show that your students then visit and experience, and vice versa.

Writing and reading artist statements allows students to make the thoughtful decisions they and other artists make when creating art for different purposes and audiences. The artist statement, as a genre, will enable writers to think through their ideas and share problems and obstacles they may have faced in expressing these through artistic expression. Writing allows students to analyze, synthesize, interpret, and reflect on their process and vision for creative work. These qualities belong in the English language arts classroom, address state, and national standards, and prepare students for the world they will one day enter as young adults and professionals.

ARTIST STATEMENT SAMPLE ASSIGNMENT

Directions: After you have completed your creative project for our book study, please write an artist statement to share your perspective and process behind the creative work. Follow these guidelines:

1. Title of creative work
2. Name of artist (that's you!)
3. Date of creative work
4. Artist process
5. The intention behind the piece
6. Creative materials

Audience: Your classmates, teacher, and school or family

Purpose: To share your thinking and process behind the creative process and experience a written genre form used in the art world and beyond. The artist statement can help your audience understand your art and feel more connected to it.

ARTIST STATEMENT MODEL TEXTS

You can have your students find examples of artist statements in these places:

1. Individual artist pages on gallery websites
2. Individual artist websites
3. Artist interviews
4. Exhibition catalogs
5. Collections of artists' writings
6. Local art galleries and exhibitions

Here are some of my favorite resources for finding models of artist statements:

1. Ten Artist Statement Examples from Modern Day Masters by Arternal, https://arternal.com/blog/10-artist-statement-examples-from-modern -day-masters/
2. 8 Artist Statements We Love by The Art League, https://www.theartleague .org/blog/2015/08/24/8-artist-statements-we-love/
3. Artist Statements from Some of the Best Landscape Photographers Nature Views by Thad M. Brown, https://natureviews.com/ landscape-photographers-artist-statements/
4. Ogden Museum of Southern Art, Coming of Age: A Teen Intern Exhibition Artist Statements, https://ogdenmuseum.org/comignofage-artist -statements/

ARTIST STATEMENT STUDENT EXAMPLE 1

Sixth-Grade Student

ARTIST: Zack

TITLE OF WORK: <u>Midnight Wars and Wonders</u>

MATERIALS: Construction Paper, Acrylic Paint, Paint Brush, My Face, and a Bobby Pin

As I look closely at my piece of artwork, I see many things. Transforming into monsters and creatures. The pain you go through to transform. The confusion, and destruction. I think of my artwork as beautifully chaotic.

If you look at everything in my piece of artwork, it looks like a bunch of paint splotches, but if you look at everything separately, things become clear. There are many angles it can be looked at from.

The steps I took to make this piece of artwork were very mixed and messy. I first tried to draw what I had originally wanted to do, and seeing that I couldn't connect with the piece, I decided to do something a little sillier: painting my face with paint and smudging it into the paper. That was my first step. My second step was pulling my hair out of my face, so I didn't get paint in my hair. I had to ask a few people to help me put it up, but eventually it worked. The third step was painting my face. It was hard to build up the courage to do it, so I asked a friend of mine to help start the process. They painted my face repeatedly to help me continue painting. I would paint my face and then roll it around on my piece of paper. Choose a new color and repeat. Once I was satisfied with my artwork, I went to the restroom and washed off my face. Which probably took about ten minutes.

A challenge I faced was, after I failed at drawing my original idea, having no idea what to draw. My original plan had failed, and I had no idea what to do. I was looking at other people's art around me when I remembered something. This is basically printing your identity on a page. And what's better to print your identity, than a stamp shaped like your face?

I liked the creative idea I thought up for how to paint my artwork. I also like that looking deeper, everyone sees something different. I disliked, however, the white background. It distracts the eye from the artwork and makes it seem unprofessional.

I learned that everyone has their own definition of artwork. Artwork doesn't always have to be a super accurate depiction of your life. It can be whatever defines you. One thing I'd like to change if I ever do this again is coloring my background completely black before applying other paints. Another thing I want to change is using bright colors, and maybe a larger color palette in general! Overall, I am really happy with my artwork, and would love to do this again sometime!

ARTIST STATEMENT STUDENT EXAMPLE 2

"overtaxed" by Stevia Ndoe

Ever since I was a child, I looked forward to my 18th birthday. I thought I would suddenly gain years of knowledge and have the power to change the world. Little did I know how difficult the year of my retirement from childhood would be.

When murmurs of quarantining were becoming a reality, my family and I were stuck. My mom, an essential worker and single parent, worked all day while my younger siblings and I attended school. On top of trying to graduate from high school, I had to be a mother for a preschooler and a grade-schooler. My 18th birthday came and went, and I was still the same Stevia.

I look at the last few months and realize this is what growing up in a global crisis looks like for low-income families. Being in quarantine made me realize how much I have been robbed of my childhood and that I've been an "adult" for the majority of my life. My photo represents waking up daily with the stress of not knowing what life is going to throw at you, but going through the motions anyway. I took this photo one morning as my siblings were still sleeping four feet away from me. The light was coming through the window so beautifully, and it was one of the few moments of silence I had experienced since March.

CHAPTER 3

Public Service Announcements

Walk the hallways of any middle or high school, and you will see students immersed in their digital worlds. Our students write, read, listen, and speak every day using their cell phones, iPads, computers, AirPods, and watches. For many writing teachers, having students tap into these digital and multimodal literacy practices offers an exciting way to break away from print-only forms of written communication. For others, it can feel challenging to bring unfamiliar or ever-evolving multimodal genre forms into the formal curriculum. Cynthia Selfe (2008) writes, "The traditional language skills of reading and writing are, in short, converging with new multimodal literacy practices and feeding off each other in ways that make learning exciting and challenging for students and teachers from kindergarten to college" (p. 86). Whether eager or anxious about including digital literacies in our writing curriculum, it is impossible to refute the importance of exposing students to multimodal forms of writing and reading. We want to tap into their own digital skills and interests as part of preparing them to be 21st-century writers.

The National Council of Teachers of English (2019), has offered position statements calling for the inclusion of multimodal literacy practices (designing through different genres of communication, including linguistic, visual, and audio) into the curriculum. The PSA is a perfect example of a genre that allows students to take up digital forms of literacy. It also requires students to write and communicate persuasively, use research, develop a sophisticated understanding of their audience and purpose, and inform or teach. Additionally, the PSA allows students to write for a public audience beyond the teacher and their peers.

The PSA is a form of multimodal communication that persuades the audience to act, much like an advertisement, but with no fees attached. PSAs promote federal, state, and local government programs or nonprofit organizations. Iconic PSAs such as "This is your brain. This is your brain on drugs" from the 1980s or "Friends don't let friends drive drunk" often help define a cultural or historical moment. For example, as the COVID-19 pandemic roared, highways had large, digitized PSAs encouraging people to get vaccinated. Health departments had launched public service campaigns and messaging to support vaccination, masking, social distancing, and testing. PSAs are used to encourage people to shift their behaviors. They can be a source of controversy and public debate. For example, a highway PSA became controversial in Arizona because of the pro-vaccine messaging. The PSA message, "Want to return to normal? Get vaccinated," outraged a state senator, who objected to it by posting a picture of it along with her opinion about it on social media. "Seen in Communist China today. Oops, I mean Arizona." The next day, the PSA was removed from all highway signs (*Arizona Republic*, 2020). This is one example of how this genre can inform and stir reaction.

PSAs have been part of written and visual communication throughout history. They were created and distributed during the suffrage movement to encourage or discourage the vote for women and during the world wars to boost morale during incredibly challenging times in the country. They have also promoted public health campaigns such as anti-smoking, hand washing, and vaccination. You may want to share a brief history of this genre with students so they can see its cultural and historical relevance along with the shifting genre expectations.

Assignment Details

PSAs generally promote positive social behaviors through information and a call to action by mixing visual or digital and textual elements that share clear and concise messaging. They are published for television and video, blogs, digital and print media, radio, and billboards. The audience and purpose often determine the medium. Some students have limited to no experience with PSAs and how they operate in the world, but many have experience reading PSAs. Ask what PSA's they have seen recently. For example, I recently asked my first-year college students what knowledge they had reading or writing PSAs. While none of them had ever created a PSA of their own, many of them referred to ones they had seen on Twitter in connection to the Black Lives Matter movement. Others shared that they had seen PSAs in support of Palestine during a recent series of bombings in Gaza, and another student shared a PSA she had seen recently advocating for Pro-Life. Hearing examples of the connections students have with this genre is a powerful way to share its relevance in their lives. I also share examples of PSAs from history, so students may see how this genre has evolved over time. A few great resources for these can be found through the *Washington Post*'s "The Top 10 PSAs of All Time," the PSA Research Center's "A Brief History of Public Service Advertising," and the Poster House's "A Brief History of PSA Posters."

The PSA is an opportunity for students to dive into the research and writing of an individual or shared topic (e.g., the unhoused population) to figure out what they believe about it and, next, what they want people to know and do differently. You can start students thinking about their topics for the PSA assignment by asking them to respond to this prompt: "Something I know and believe about that I want others to know and believe is _____."

A sentence starter is a quick and effective way to have students begin brainstorming topics and thinking about issues they care about deeply. Instead of having students choose the topic, you might want to select a current topic in the community that students see or hear about frequently or that feels particularly relevant in the present moment. Or you could pick an issue directly related to a book you are reading as a class, so the writing of the PSA is a direct extension of the reading curriculum.

When inviting students to create PSAs, you can offer the choice between making a print, video, audio, or combined video and audio PSA. This gives students some ownership of presenting their topics and allows them to play with and learn about various digital tools and design elements. You can also keep things simple and have students create analog PSA posters to display at school or in the community (see PSA Student Example). An example of a PSA assignment for sixth–12th grades offers three choices in mode. Students can create a written and visual analog poster, a digital PSA video, or a recorded PSA audio (see PSA Sample Assignment). This may be modified to fit grade level and purpose and to include only one of the options for the final product if this feels more manageable in terms of teaching and assessment.

Reading Connection

Immersing students in reading a collection of print, video, and audio PSAs exposes them to various forms and uses of digital tools. You can enlist students to search for one of each kind connected to a topic they care about, and you can provide models for your class to read (see Model Texts).

Students can examine model PSAs using a series of rhetorical and analytical questions to gain a sense of the audience, purpose, conventions, and organizational structures. It works best to have students do this close analysis with three examples of the kind of PSA they want to end up creating, either print, audio, or video versions. You can also group students based on the PSA form they have selected and then have them do this close reading and analysis of PSA in their form together instead of individually.

Questions to Guide Rhetorical and Analytical
Close Reading of PSAs

1. What is the purpose?
2. Who is the intended audience? How do you know this?
3. Who is the author or sponsor?
4. How was the PSA shared publicly?
5. What are the strengths and weaknesses of the PSA? Explain.
6. What appeals does the author target (e.g., emotion, reason, character)?
7. How does the author present the information or make an argument?
8. What kind of information is shared?
9. What digital or print tools does the author utilize? What kind of media?
10. How is the genre organized or displayed?
11. How does the PSA tell a story?
12. What elements make up the PSA (e.g., facts or data, images, music, voice-over)?

Another option is to have students closely examine the resources you provide to figure out what genre elements make up a successful PSA.

You can also have students start the PSA unit by exploring PSA examples from websites or resources you provide and then figuring out the genre through their observations. Here is an example of the directions Heidi, a high school teacher in Phoenix, Arizona, created and uses with her students to get started thinking about PSAs as a genre and reading model texts:

PSA Exploration Activity

1. Click on the resources tab and locate the document labeled PSA Websites. Open the PSA documents.
2. Click on each website and write important information, things that stand out, trends, etc.
3. Go beyond the first page where necessary and absorb as much information regarding Public Service Announcements as possible.
4. When you finish looking at all the sites and writing down information on your brain dump map, compare your information in a group of 3–4 students.
5. In your group, create a definition of a PSA and write it down in the space provided.
6. Create a checklist of essential items you think should be included to create a compelling and complete PSA.

Writing Workshop Tip:
Storyboarding and Script Writing

Students benefit from time to map out and plan their PSAs through storyboarding. You can provide a sheet of paper with four to six numbered boxes (the length and complexity vary depending on grade level) to storyboard their PSA (Storyboard Template for Audio and Visual PSAs). The parts will vary depending on the kind of PSA the student creates. For example, if they create a video, each box can represent a different panel or part of the video shoot. If the PSA is audio, the students can use the six boxes to map out the visuals and the text or script to go with the visuals. Students can think about audio or visual components, text, and special effects (e.g., music, fade-out/in) and plan for each in the boxes. They may also do this with sticky notes on poster paper. Or students can use digital spaces for storyboarding like StoryboardThat or Adobe Spark.

One of my first-year college students drew a cartoon-style PSA about suicide prevention. Her storyboard was a rough panel sketch of the images and words she wanted to make for the PSA, and her final PSA had a graphic novel-like feel (see PSA Student Example). Another student created a quick sketch of the poster she planned for her PSA about the importance of therapy to support adolescents and college students (see Figure 3.1, Sample Student Storyboard for Analog PSA Poster).

Providing class time for students to storyboard allows them opportunities to draft and solidify plans with the input of their peers. As with most writing, this does not have to be a solo process. Bouncing ideas off one another helps students generate ideas and avoid writer's block. You can also wander the room and check in with students to help support their drafting and planning or redirect them if their plans are too ambitious.

It's also helpful to show your drafting and planning examples for any written genre you teach. Here is an example of a storyboard for a PSA a high school teacher, Sara, created to share with her students. The storyboard shares her plan for a video PSA with music and voiceover focused on

FIGURE 3.1 Sample Student Storyboard for Analog PSA Poster

FIGURE 3.2 Teacher Storyboard Example for Digital PSA

the need for secondary students to read more diverse books. The drawing includes a sketch of the kinds of images she wants to have, and she also includes the song lyrics she wants to add and some of the voice-over text.

As students storyboard their PSAs, you can ask them to keep in mind these questions:

- What's the story?
- What's my hook?
- What evidence do I have? Is there a quote I can use and cite?
- What data, information, or facts can I share?
- How will I get my audience to relate (pathos)?
- What's the call to action?

Digital Tools

Students' digital tools for the PSA assignment will vary depending on the medium they choose and their access to devices at school (e.g., iPad vs. computers or cell phones). Many middle and high school students have their cell phones or access to iPads through school. In this case, I encourage them to use the camera or video feature on these to shoot original videos or photographs for their PSAs. They can use iMovie or Clips (by Apple) or Windows MovieMaker to shoot and edit a film. Also they can use the voice recorder on any cell phone or iPad to record audio for voice-over or the PSA audio.

No matter the PSA, students will want to incorporate photographs to support their story or argument. You can encourage students to take their own photos if they love to do that. This is also an excellent way of inviting them to use their cell phone photo collection for a legitimate academic purpose, although they should obtain permission from people whose photos they take (see the Author's Note on privacy and permission). If students do not want to take their own pictures, there are several great resources of Creative Commons photos to have students choose from, such as Pics4learning.com and Photosforclass.com (but see the Author's Note on Creative Commons licenses). Be sure to review your school's policies on using student images and using social media in the classroom. You also want to make sure all students are set up for success equally, so every student has the tech resources they need to create their PSAs at school. You will want to secure permission slips if needed. Glogster EDU (edu.glogster.com) is a helpful resource that enables students to brainstorm the overall concept of their PSA in a multimodal form in the drafting process.

Extensions

Once students have finalized their PSAs, various digital tools or spaces are available to share their work with a broader audience. Here are suggestions for creative ways to share the PSAs within your classroom community and beyond:

- **Class Blog.** If you have a class blog or webpage, post the PSAs.
- **Digital Portfolio.** SeeSaw, which is a digital portfolio site (awesome for sixth grade).
- **Digital Collaboration Board.** Flipgrid or Padlet.com. Flipgrid is a video tool that allows students to share their work, comment, and collaborate. Padlet is a web-based digital collaborative board. You can add notes (like digital sticky notes) along with pictures and videos. You can invite your class to create a PSA Padlet board and have them add their videos, audio, and or

posters. You can also open up the project with a broader audience by sharing the Padlet with families, so they have access to all the class's PSAs.

- **Class YouTube, TeacherTube, or Vimeo.** Create a class YouTube channel (you can make it private and just share the link with parents or create a grade-level PSA contest for students to share and receive feedback on their work).

- **Student Media Contests and Events.** There are opportunities for students to participate in film festivals, media challenges (check out KQED Youth Media Challenges https://learn.kqed.org/challenges/teachers), and public service campaigns.

- **Class Screening.** Invite parents, roll out the red carpet and have a movie screening of all the student videos. This is so much fun! You can share these at an open house or curriculum night or screen the videos and digital posters in the cafeteria, classroom, or other school spaces.

- **School Newsletter or Morning Announcements.** Ask the administration if you can have your students' PSAs included in the newsletter or morning announcements as examples of student writing. Share issues that matter to youth.

PSA MODEL TEXTS

Great resources for high quality PSAs that work well across secondary grades include:

- The Ad Council Website (https://www.adcouncil.org/)
- The National Youth Anti-Drug Media Campaign (https://drugfree.org/drug-and-alcohol-news/national-youth-anti-drug-media-campaign-launches-new-ad-campaign/)
- The Environmental Protection Agency (https://www.epa.gov/natural-disasters/public-service-announcements-about-emergencies-and-disasters)

Here are samples of PSAs that relate to teen issues and have been successful in engaging students in the analysis of this genre in a variety of forms:

- Video: NBC's PSA for Teen Driving
- Audio: CDC Radio: Handwashing for General Public PSA (:15) on Apple Podcasts
- Print: PETA PSA Campaigns

PSA POSTER STUDENT EXAMPLES

Materials: poster paper and colorful pens

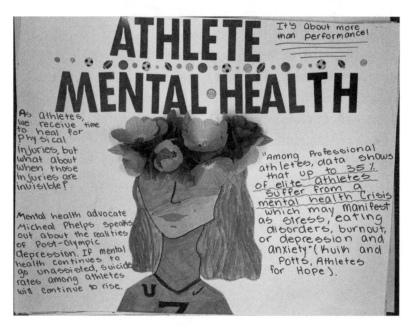

PSA SAMPLE ASSIGNMENT

Purpose: The writer will create a Public Service Announcement (PSA) based on a topic (self-selected or determined by the teacher). The final PSA should either be written and visual text, video, or audio. The writer will select a topic and determine an appropriate and accessible, real audience for the PSA. The writer will use the PSA to move people to action using: (1) research; (2) a combination of text, image, and voice recording; and (3) appeal to reason, emotion, or personal responsibility about this issue.

Genre: The genre is a Public Service Announcement (PSA). PSAs are a multimodal genre, which means they use different forms of written and digital communication, including text, images, video, and audio. PSAs communicate a message for the common good. They often share information to move people to action. PSAs are brief and attention-grabbing. They allow readers to quickly and easily digest an idea or information to act on it.

Audience: A public organization or community group (TBD by student based on topic and with the support of the teacher).

Sources: Make sure that the final PSA includes the following information to give credit for your source material:

- Copyright: Identify the owner of any work that you incorporated into your infographic, including any graphics or visuals, and state whether there are restrictions on the further publication or other use of that material (see the Author's Note on copyright, and in particular, about terms of use and Creative Commons licenses)
- Source data, so anyone can check your facts
- Original image or article address, so anyone who sees the image can find the original
- Citations for all external sources using MLA or APA format, typically placed at the bottom of the infographic, or a tagline for a sponsor (someone supporting or paying for the PSA)

CONTINUED

PSA Genre Elements

1. They are brief. Print PSAs are typically one to two pages, and video/digital PSAs are around one minute in length.
2. They target a real audience.
3. They incorporate research.
4. They use media (digital, audio, visual).
5. They include some combination or selection of images, written text, sounds, music, sound effects, voice-over, headlines, title(s), or quote(s) (see the Author's Note on copyright).
6. They make an argument or tell a story to encourage action or change.
7. They often appeal to emotion.
8. They include acknowledging the sources and supporting teachers or sponsor(s) in references or in a tagline at the end of the video, digital, or written document.
9. If the PSA is a video, it must include voice-over commentary.

Format: Written PSAs are typically designed to fit one to two pages. Video or Audio PSAs are 30–60 seconds. Design the PSA with your final viewing size in mind. Fonts, color choices, and design elements will vary.

STORYBOARD TEMPLATE: AUDIO AND VISUAL PSAS

Instructions: Please use this template to map out, design, and script your audio or visual PSA.

Visual: Image or camera directions	Audio
Scene 1	Scene 1
Transition:	
Scene 2	Scene 2
Transition:	
Scene 3	Scene 3
Transition:	
Scene 4	Scene 4

PSA STUDENT EXAMPLE

First-Year College Student

Don't wait, speak up.
Do your part in preventing suicide

References

Innes, S. (2021). State drops Covid-19 vaccine freeway message that Arizona senator likens to communism. *The Arizona Republic*. Retrieved February 23, 2022 from : https://www.azcentral.com/story/news /politics /arizona/2021/05/11/arizona-drops-adot-covid-19-message-kelly-town send-likened-communism/5041631001/

National Council of Teachers of English. (2019). Definition of literacy in a digital age. Retrieved February 22, 2022 from https://ncte.org/statement/ nctes-definition-literacy-digital-age/

Selfe, R. J., & Selfe, C. L. (2008). Convince me! Valuing multimodal literacies and composing public service announcements. *Theory into Practice*, *47*(2), 83–92.

CHAPTER 4

Infographics

Infographics are "visual presentations of complex data and information presented in a compact and easily understood display" (Anderson, Bishop, & Cross, 2018, p. 1). Writers use infographics to present large quantities of information in an easy-to-read format, to define a series of terms in an appealing way, and to invite readers to focus on a specific aspect of research. This genre involves a combination of design, research, data summary, and presentation. Infographics are found everywhere in today's world. I keep a running tally in the classroom of all the places we find this genre in our lives beyond the classroom. Students come back with examples from sports games, doctor's offices, election results and voter pamphlets, city transit stations, news articles, and social media. My own mail on a single day included two: a "Suggested Water Use" infographic to help hikers determine the amount of water to bring on a desert hike, and another in my electric bill explaining ways to save energy in the home.

Infographics are three times more likely to be shared on social media than any other kind of content (Krystian, 2016). Almost all forms of media and digital communication utilize infographics to distribute information quickly and widely to audiences; thus, they represent an essential genre for preparing students as readers and writers in the 21st century. I have been assigninged infographics for a few years now and my students love writing in this genre. They find it a relief to write because it is such a departure from the kind of writing they are often asked to do in school. I first assigned infographics because I saw them as a wonderful introduction to a multimodal writing form. The infographic assignment fit this goal perfectly, but I soon found it does so much more. Writers use this genre to make arguments, teach, and inform. Infographics can also be used to tell a story. For those of us working in schools and districts that are emphasizing the importance of argumentative writing, this is a way to open the writing curriculum to include many methods for students to make arguments, synthesize research, and share information beyond the formal essay.

Infographics may be used across all ages and disciplines:

1. To expose students to a digital writing form
2. To get them out of the routine of writing in a formulaic or too familiar five-paragraph essay
3. As an alternative to traditional presentation tools (e.g., PowerPoint)
4. To make an argument and share research
5. As a reading response or reading assessment tool

As a multimodal writing form, infographics invite students to draw on skills they have honed in their digital lives by incorporating visual and textual elements to present and share information.

We tend to think of the infographic as an innovation of our highly digitized and multimodal world. However, this writing form is not new. Its origins date back to ancient times when people created cave paintings Physician John Snow used an infographic to trace London's 1854 cholera outbreak to one water pump by charting incidences of the disease on a map (Rogers, 2013). Sociologist W. E. B. DuBois produced hand-drawn graphics in 1899 to share data from his studies of African American life and to depict trends in connection to slavery, residential patterns, and control of economic assets (Anderson, 2018).

You can introduce infographics using examples suitable and adaptable for secondary students (see Suggested Readings and Video on the History of Infographics) to show how this genre has changed throughout history. Whenever possible, you want to remind students of the ways writing is situated in context and history and how writing shifts with context and social purpose. Humans create new communication tools as needed to convey our thoughts most effectively to one another.

Infographics require attention to the rhetorical situation as well as to concision. The writer must think about who they are communicating to, why, and for what purpose(s). They must get their message and information across clearly and quickly. The genre also requires the thoughtful use of visual and textual elements. For many students, the visual and design aspect of this genre is something they have a great deal of experience with as consumers of information, but much less experience with as writers. It helps to provide a framework for students to think about the choices they make with regards to planning their visual and design choices.

Here are questions I have students use to help frame their thinking as they plan and draft their infographics:

- Do you want to present information in chronological order (order of time or importance), in a spatial sequence (using charts, symbols, characters), using quantitative information (numbers and data), or some combination of these three?
- Think about the way the pieces of the infographic work together to create a clear and cohesive message. Do you move from big ideas to small? Do you help the reader understand how to read through headings, bold text, or color choices?

It is also helpful to provide students with the typically included genre elements of an infographic, which are also the elements you may choose to use for assessment: (1) a direct, straightforward title (2) use of a variety of visuals, colors, and texts to present information, (3) data and facts, (4) data that is visualized with texts and images, and (5) use of color and contrast to make material readable.

The *New York Times* also outlines key components of successful infographics: (1) easily understandable information that helps the reader find or do something, (2) integrates words and images in a fluid and dynamic way, (3) stands alone and is self-explanatory, (4) reveals information that others cannot easily find or that was hidden, (5) makes for easy and fast understanding, and (6) is understandable for a wide audience (Schulten, 2010).

Assignment Details

The infographic may be assigned as a stand-alone writing assignment in connection to research or as a reading response. After students practice a low-stakes infographic on a topic of their choice, I assign a more formal project, either in response to reading, in connection to a research project, or as part of a literary unit. The writing assignment is typically a way of sharing research on topics students are exploring within the context of the larger curriculum. For example, if students are working toward writing a research paper, I ask them to include an infographic as a way of first sharing the research. Then I have them embed the infographic in the final research paper as an attachment or sidebar. You can also assign infographics as a response to reading as a whole class, in literature circles, or through independent reading (see Sample Infographic Assignment).

Heather O'Loughlin, the English Language Arts (ELA) teacher in my writing project whose PSA checklist is in Chapter 3, teaches high school juniors and seniors. She has her students create infographics in response to informational articles. For example, she asked her students to read an article from the *HuffPost News* (2022) called "Target is Tracking You and Changing Prices Based on Your Location," by Casey Bond. The article is full of data and visuals to help explain the pricing strategies Target uses to track customers based on their location and shopping habits (e.g., online vs. in person). After having students read and annotate the article, she then asked students to summarize the article and answer two questions: (1) What are your thoughts about variable pricing and (2) What surprised you about this article and why? Finally, she asked students to create infographics that worked to summarize the article, share their opinion or reaction to variable pricing as a marketing practice, and include their reaction to the piece. Students not only loved this assignment for its relevance to their lives as consumers, but because of the way they could incorporate visual and design elements into their written communication (at the end of this chapter, I've included a infographic example created by a teacher).

I assign infographics to accompany in-person or digital (Flipgrid or Voice-Thread) book talks. Students read a book of choice connected to a theme or topic we are studying and then create an oral book talk and an infographic to teach others about the book and to reflect and share their response to it (see the Sample Infographic Book Summary and Book Talk Assignment at the end of the chapter). Students in one of my methods courses on teaching writing, who are ELA teachers, created infographics based on books on teaching secondary writing that they read for the class (see Sample Infographic). They used these as examples with their own students when teaching infographics in response to reading books of choice. I invite you to use this example with students or to create your own based on something you have been reading.

The great thing about the infographic is that it can be taught in connection to almost any aspect of the ELA curriculum. The possibilities for incorporating this genre into your curriculum are endless.

Reading Connection

Part of familiarizing students with the genre expectations of infographics is spending time having them consider the audience, purpose, and repeated patterns in this genre form. An easy way to start seeing the visual design choices of authors in creating arguments and in delivering information is to ask them to read a variety of examples. You can share a selection of infographics that span disciplines and careers to highlight the ways this writing form is used through advertising, public relations, medicine, and so on. I typically share four to five compelling and well-organized infographics. This gives students examples of ways writers display data. Published infographics from a variety of sources and contexts show how visual and textual choices can make or break the accessibility of an infographic for readers. You may also provide students with strong examples of infographics other students have created at their grade level, so they see peer work as models along with professional examples. Justin, a teacher in my writing project, invites his sixth-grade students to practice creating infographics based on social, political, or environmental issues that matter deeply to them. His students often select lofty topics like endangered marine wildlife, global warming, childhood obesity, and eating disorders. His main goal in this first practice exercise is to have students use at least one outside source and cite it and use facts in the infographic.

Close reading of infographics also gives students the opportunity to identify and articulate effective and ineffective visual design choices and problematic or powerful displays of information. One close reading exercise to do along with students is to highlight and annotate the moves writers make in creating their infographics. For example, students can highlight the ways writers relay facts or information. Or students can focus on visual design elements writers use to guide their reader, such as color choice, spacing, layout, and font choices. Students often take note of the ways writers use images to help guide the reader's eye or attention. Students highlight things like arrows or flow charts that take the reader's focus from one text box to another in a particular order. We also talk about use of color contrast and fonts that help guide the reader and communicate big and small ideas. Students can use a different highlighter to mark evidence as they read a collection of model infographics. Along with encouraging the act of visually annotating the models, you can invite students to respond to some guiding questions to support their close reading:

Questions and Instructions for Close Reading of Infographics

- Who is the target audience for the infographic?
- What is the story or information the author shares?
- What is the takeaway message or "So what?" for this piece?
- What are the visual aspects of this piece?
- Choose a digital tool to create the graphic (see Digital Tools).
- Look for royalty-free digital images.
- What stylistic elements do you want to highlight (e.g., headers/subheaders, fonts, colors)?

Another resource for infographics is InformationisBeautiful.net. This is a fantastic collection of infographics spanning all disciplines and topics. For an extension or homework assignment, you can ask students to find two to three infographics on this site and use your close reading list to read, compare the different writing and design choices, and reflect on the kinds of choices they want to make in creating their own infographics.

Digital Tools

After introducing the infographic, students need time to practice this genre using digital tools with low stakes attached. You can offer 15–20 minutes for students to create a simple infographic about a topic of their choice connected to an issue they care about in their neighborhood or community. Here are some instructions to help guide this quick practice exercise:

- Choose a topic: anything you can quickly research
- Pew Research is helpful for easy facts
- Visualize the graphic and don't start from scratch*
- Create for 20 minutes
- Share in small (in-person or breakout) groups

This is a step you can take more time with by having students create an infographic prototype using old fashioned paper, scissors, glue sticks, and other craft items. After they create their prototypes, you can ask them to write out their thought process to communicate their design choices. This makes their thinking visible to themselves and others before diving into the digital realm.

Digital Tools to Create Infographics

Infogram: a free (at the basic level) visualization tool to help design infographics.

Piktochart: a visual content maker for creating charts and infographics. This tool is free with an account (easy to make with an email address), but is aimed at professional users, meaning it is a bit more complex than Canva (see below) and some of the other digital platforms.

Easel.ly: a simple and free infographic maker tool with templates.

Venngage: a free infographic maker with templates to choose from to support design.

Canva: a free graphic design platform with templates for creating infographics and other visual design presentations.

Picmonkey: an online photo and editing service with infographic templates. May be accessed from a web browser or through a mobile app; allows a free trial usage.

These tools provide templates and design choices that help students create the genre without having to worry too much about complicated formatting. These are also the digital tools writers use when creating the infographic genre. Digital tools are always evolving and students often find new resources to add to the list. You can have students dive into using one of the digital tools to create their practice infographics, or they can practice drafting the infographic on paper and then transfer the plan to a digital space.

My classes create their practice infographics on topics of their choice like skateboarding, tattoo design, voter registration, and meditation. One student, an avid bread baker, was determined to continue her bread baking hobby when she moved to the college dormitory as a first-year college student. She created an infographic explaining how to bake bread while living in a dorm. Heather O'Loughlin, the high school English teacher we met previously, has her tenth-grade students create infographics as part of a unit she teaches about activists and changemakers. One of her students created an infographic about Pablo Recalde, a former professional soccer player who is now an activist. He works in connection to the World Food Program to help feed people in Darfur.

Writing Workshop Tip: Peer Review

As teachers of writing, we typically use peer review in our classrooms to encourage students to read one another's work and to give them support and feedback at the draft stage. Offering a peer review session in class gives students a chance to pinpoint several focus areas and improvements for their infographics. Peer reviews provide valuable insight into the successes and failures of their work and give students a practice run at printing the infographics to check for sizing, font, and colors that make their texts accessible and successful to the reader. Students' peer feedback should move beyond surface-level editing (e.g., spelling, title changes, grammar) and instead focus on content, design, and organizational elements. Through peer review, students can begin to see how others read their work and if the content and design elements allow the reader to follow the author's line of thinking.

You can invite students to take part in peer review in small groups or partners or online using Google Docs, Canvas, or Blackboard. You can offer a few guiding questions to support students in giving one another substantive feedback.

Infographic Peer Review Questions

After reviewing your classmates' infographic, please respond to three or four of the questions below:

1. What really stands out to you about this infographic?
2. Who is the audience for this infographic?
3. What is the purpose?
4. What is missing? Or what do you want to know more about?
5. How does the infographic invite you to engage with the topic? What are the main themes, topics, etc. that the infographic emphasizes?
6. What is most visually appealing about the infographic?
7. Which visual elements need adjustment? What do you think these adjustments should be?
8. What are the overall strengths of the infographic?
9. What are the overall areas for improvement or revision?

Creating an infographic using the digital tools is thoroughly satisfying and rewarding because the templates create a polished and presentable image with minimal effort. What you want students to think about in revising their work are the nuances that go into creating successful visual and textual communication within the parameters of this genre form. You will find that students have great instincts in peer review and often give one another the exact kinds of revision suggestions you might give. You can encourage students throughout their writing process to trust and take up the feedback of their peers. You may also provide students support with general tips that consider the kinds of issues you've seen students struggle with in connection to this genre. Here are the kinds of general suggestions I provide in supporting revision from the first draft of the infographic to the final:

1. **Audience:** Directly state the audience for the infographic or book you are presenting through the infographic. What will the intended audience gain from reading this infographic or from reading the book you are presenting in the infographic?
2. **Detail vs. Brevity:** Infographics are meant to be brief, but make sure you have enough content. Represent the topic clearly. Remember, an infographic is a written genre designed to make the reading of information

quick, accessible, and easy. This means you can pack a big punch in terms of content by using relatively few words.

3. **Design:** Think about the template you used. Is that layout the best for the information you want to convey? A long and narrow infographic is great for a list or a very linear text, but not all texts are linear. Consider the colors and graphics. Do they help the reader engage with the infographic?

Infographics give students an opportunity to practice a multimodal genre and to move away from the traditional 5-paragraph essay. This genre requires text and images and pushes students to think in new ways about what counts as writing in our digital world. It also gives them a chance to use digital and design elements to enhance and complement their written text. Infographics offer a layering of ideas and form and give students practice summarizing and making sense of information to share with their audience in an easy-to-read and visually appealing format. This genre is also brief. As teachers of writing, we often feel that we don't have enough time to give justice to teaching the genre elements or the different parts of the writing process. Because this genre can easily be paired with reading or in connection to research, it can be included without a huge time commitment. If you want to take a step further to use the infographic as a civic action project, ask students to share their infographics on social media or around campus or even out in the community. The best part about teaching this genre is that students love the chance to play with digital tools and use visual and design elements as they write.

SUGGESTED READINGS AND VIDEOS ON
THE HISTORY OF INFOGRAPHICS

- Krystian, M. (2016, May 10). *A brief look at the fascinating history of infographics*. Infogram. https://infogram.com/blog/a-brief-look-at-the-fascinating -history-of-infographics/
- Smiciklas, M. (2012). *The power of infographics: Using pictures to communicate and connect with your audience.* Indianapolis, IN: Que Biz-Tech.
- Lima, M. (2015). "A visual history of knowledge." TED Talk. http://www .ted.com/talks/view/id/2296
- McCandless, D. (2010). "The beauty of data visualization," TED Talk. https://www.ted.com/talks/david_mccandless_the_beauty_of_data_ visualization?language=en

INFOGRAPHIC MODEL TEXTS

- **Diversity in Children's Books**
  This infographic shares the ways people from diverse backgrounds are represented through children's books. https://readings park.wordpress.com/2019/06/19/picture-this-diversity-in-childrens-books-2018-infographic/

- **How to Save Water in the Yard This Summer**
  A visual of specific strategies for saving water in the summer months. https://srpnet.com/water/arizona-water.aspx?utm_campaign =124961&utm_medium=ps&utm_source=goog&utm_content =genrl&utm_id=2278528438&utm_term=%7Bkeyword%7D&https:// srpnet.com/water/arizona-water.aspx

- **The History of Gaming**
  This infographic shares a timeline of the history of video gaming. https://www.historydegree.net/history-of-gaming/

- **Women in Sports**
  A history of women's inclusion in professional sports. https://www.athleticbusiness.com/operations/programming/ article/15148130/infographic-the-evolution-of-womens-sports

- **COVID-19 Vaccines**
  Information about current vaccines available to protect against COVID-19. https://www.hopkinsmedicine.org/health/conditions-and-diseases/ coronavirus/coronavirus-vaccines-infographic

- **If Facebook Were a Country**
  Visual depiction of Facebook use in different countries. https://www.visualcapitalist.com/map-facebook-path-social-network -domination/

- **Cell Phone Etiquette Around the World**
  Explanation of different cell phone habits based on geographic location. https://www.leaflanguages.org/folium-cell-phone-etiquette-around-the -world-via-best-infographics/

- **Daily Infographic**
  A collection of quality infographics about a wide range of topics. http:// www.dailyinfographic.com/

SAMPLE INFOGRAPHIC ASSIGNMENT

Purpose: The writer summarizes, synthesizes, and shares information about a topic (self-selected or determined by the teacher) using an infographic. The final written product is a detailed infographic using and citing outside sources. In the infographic, the writer reports on a topic and shares what it is and why it matters to the intended audience. Included are major themes or information about the topic, valuable ideas or practices, and useful data or knowledge. Additional information, if relevant, may cite strengths and weaknesses of the work being done locally, regionally, nationally, or internationally in relation to this topic, groups and organizations that support this work, or questions that arise from reading and learning about this issue, and so on.

Genre: This is an infographic. Infographics are a visual and textual genre that allow readers to digest information and data quickly and easily. Strong infographics are informative, but they are also persuasive and attention grabbing.

Audience: Peers, teacher, and/or community organization or space where the infographic is to be placed.

Sources: Make sure that the final infographic includes the following information to give credit for your source material:

- **Copyright:** Identify the owner of any work that you incorporated into your infographic, including any graphics or visuals, and state whether there are restrictions on the further publication or other use of that material (see the Author's Note on copyright, and in particular, about terms of use and Creative Commons licenses)
- **Source data:** so anyone can check your facts
- **Original image/article address:** so anyone who sees the image can find the original
- **Citations for all external sources (using MLA or APA format):** these are typically placed at the bottom of the infographic
- **Required genre elements:**
  - Title/header

- A clear and concise argument or message
- Appealing and effective color scheme
- Headers and subheaders (if needed)
- Visuals (e.g., charts, graphs, images, words) that fit the message and communicate information clearly (use visuals from sources like Creative Commons, but be sure to read the particular license associated with the visual you want to use; see the Author's Note on copyright)
- Data (e.g., statistics, facts, graphs) used to communicate the information, argument, or message

Format: Infographics are typically designed to fit a single page. Design the infographic with your final viewing size in mind. Fonts, color choices, and design elements will vary.

TEACHER INFOGRAPHIC EXAMPLE

DAILY TASKS FOR TEACHING DURING COVID

Create online content for students.

Lessons should be uploaded into the Learning Management System your school uses. The content needs to be accessible for virtual and hybrid students. This is important in the instance that a student gets sick and needs to unexpectedly switch from hybrid to virtual, or if you become sick unexpectedly. In addition, you need to make sure that all of the pages, assignments, and activities are published correctly so students can complete them.

Take Daily Attendance and Keep Detailed Records for Contact Tracing

Accurate attendance needs to be taken correctly in a variety of methods, depending on your school's policies. An example of an attendance taking policy includes: submitting attendance via Synergy (an online attendance program), keeping a record of which students were in-person during their hybrid days, keeping a record of where each student who is in the hybrid model sits and who they sit by, and checking an attendance form for students who were not able to meet virtually but completed work.

Santize the Classroom Frequently

Many schools have sanitizing protocols in place such as: spraying the desks with an approved solution, wiping down high touch surfaces, deep cleaning days on asynchronous days, and providing hand sanitizer in all of the areas students frequent, especially classrooms.

Verify Students are Following Covid Protocols

Schools also have a variety of protocols in place such as: required mask wearing, sitting in assigned areas only, assigned walkways for specific directions of traveling from each class, lunch time protocols, and social distancing during lunch. While administration and security are

REILLY,KATIE. (2020, AUGUST 26). THIS IS WHAT IT'S LIKE TO BE A TEACHER DURING THE CORONAVIRUS PANDEMIC.TIME.HTTPS://TIME.COM/5883584/TEACHERS-CORONAVIRUS/

SCHWARTZ,S. (2020, AUGUST 5). CLASSROOM ROUTINES MUST CHANGE. HERE'S WHAT TEACHING LOOKS LIKE UNDER COVID-19. EDUCATION WEEK. HTTPS://WWW.EDWEEK.ORG/EW/ARTICLES/2020/08/06/CLASSROOM-ROUTINES-HAVE-TO-CHANGE-HERES-WHAT.HTML

Source: Nicole Nava

INFOGRAPHIC AND AUDIO BOOK TALK: ASSIGNMENT GUIDE IN RESPONSE TO READING

For this assignment, you can ask students to respond to a text they have read in class (e.g., a book the whole class read, a book of choice, a short story or essay) as a book study to share with you and classmates. Students create an infographic based on a book they read over the course of a few weeks. At the end of the three-week period, they create an infographic with the following components:

- The book title and author
- Major themes or topics in the book
- Valuable ideas or practices described
- The intended audience
- What you valued about the book and why

While I let students know the bulleted points above are required, they may add additional information including strengths and weaknesses of the text, how the text connects to other things we have read in class or books they have read on their own, questions that arise from the text, and so on. Along with the infographic, I ask students to create an audio book talk.

Video Book Talk

This part of the project will be a video book talk created in VoiceThread or Flipgrid or a technology that works best for your school context and students. This should be approximately two minutes in length. Have students use the audio or video function in VoiceThread (your choice) and do the following:

- Imagine you are talking to a friend, and you have two minutes to share what you know about the book you read and convince the friend to read it.
- Share the book and title as well as the most important themes, ideas, insights, and so on that would motivate a friend to read the book to impact their life in some way.

Comment on two peers' threads. In your comment, tell your peer something interesting you learned about the book from the book talk.

References

Anderson, Erin. (2018). Anderson, E. K., Raven, B. & Cross, N. (2019) Dealing with data: Instructing with infographics in an undergraduate sociology course. *College Teaching, 67*(1), 36–49.

Arizona State Parks and Trails. (2021). Hiking safety. https://azstateparks .com/hiking-safety

Bond, C. (2022). Target is tracking you and changing prices based on your location. *HuffPost News.* https://www.huffpost.com/entry/ target-tracking-location-changing-prices_1_603fd12bc5b6ff75ac410a38.

Dick, M. (2020). *The infographic: A history of data graphics in news and communications.* MIT Press.

Krystian, M. (2017, August 10). 12 most common types of infographics. Infogram. https://infogram.com/blog/12-types-of-infographics/

Krystian, M. (2016, May 10). A brief look at the fascinating history of infographics. Infogram. https://infogram.com/blog/a-brief-look-at-the-fascinating -history-ofinfographics/

Jones, R. (2013). John Snow's data journalism: The cholera map that changed the world. *The Guardian.* https://www.theguardian.com/news/ datablog/2013/mar/15/john-snow-cholera-map

Schulten, K. (2010). Teaching with infographics: A student project model. *New York Times.* https://learning.blogs.nytimes.com/2010/08/27/ teaching-with-infographics-a-student-project-model/

CHAPTER 5

The Op-Ed

Op-ed pieces help readers become informed on social issues by showing them opposing views, new or unique ways of thinking about a topic, and up-to-date research and experts. Any of these may result in readers pursuing an interest or focus. This genre lends itself to students conducting independent research seeking to back their claims and ground their issues in context and information. It is a perfect genre to take frustration and turn it into action. Readers generally love argument and opinion and turn to this genre daily in newspapers, in social media feeds, and through blogs and radio.

I began writing op-ed articles for my local paper, *The Oregonian*, when I was in my first years as a high school teacher living in Oregon. I was frustrated with reading education articles each week about what wasn't working in the city's so-called failing schools. I wanted to see writing that also reflected the joy and successes that come with teaching. I started writing opinion pieces about the everyday work I conducted with students and sent my articles to the paper. To my surprise, some were published, and they even mailed me a small check for each accepted piece. Not only did I get to see my voice and ideas reflected in the news, but teacher friends from other schools deeply appreciated the perspective that more closely aligned with their own experiences. You do not have to be an op-ed writer to bring this genre to your students, although I invite you to write along with your students as they create their pieces and send them out in the world.

Some op-eds make an argument in a story or narrative form. Others use formal research, data, and facts to make a claim and support it. Students can use different rhetorical appeals to make their case depending on the topic and their relationship to it. For example, when I write op-ed pieces about my teaching, I call upon my experience in the classroom. The examples I can render from my students and my years in the classroom are far more powerful than any statistic or cited research article. I use facts and conduct research, but when I need either to back up or emphasize what I know firsthand, I turn to my experience. We want our students to realize their perspective and knowledge carries weight and can be just as effective as external voices.

The op-ed has essential components, as shown below. These elements are introduced as mini lessons that can become assessed components at the end of the writing unit.

1. **A Strong Topic and Theme.** Consider personal experiences, issues of importance, or influential individuals and how they relate to the overarching theme. What do the experiences have to do with the big idea?
2. **A Clear Claim and Counterclaim.** Take a stand on an issue and back it up. Your claim is your thesis or main idea. Your counterclaim is an acknowledgement of another perspective.
3. **Use of Evidence.** Include experience from your own life. Embed outside texts and events or ideas; explicitly reference outside sources (e.g., infographics, statistics, evidence from expertise and lived experience). References to research, data, and current events are usually included.
4. **Effective Lead.** Consider effective techniques for a leading sentence, such as a beginning with a powerful quote, a series of questions, or a compelling anecdote.
5. **Call to Action.** Step outside the claim and evidence to emphasize the significance of the topic and lesson learned. Share why the story represents the writer's unique interests and potential contributions to a specific audience.

As students read sample op-eds to gain familiarity with the genre, you want to include examples written by adolescents. For example, a former ninth-grader, Mary, wrote an op-ed about the importance of funding public libraries. In her piece, she drew from her experience as a library-going kid and avid reader, which supported her claim that libraries need more funding. Tamsin, a tenth-grader in Tempe, Arizona, wrote and published an op-ed about the importance of mask-wearing during the COVID-19 pandemic. In her piece (2021) in the *Arizona Capital Times*, "The Choice to Wear Masks in School Can Come Down to Pimples or Public Health," she draws on her experience wearing masks to school and volleyball practice. Along with her personal experiences, she references state law and shares how the state legislators met to ensure masking mandates in the state. Her piece is a reaction to the no-mask mandate and an argument against it.

One of my first-year college students, wrote an op-ed for the university newspaper about transphobia on the college campus, "It's Not Trans Students' Responsibility to Demand Respect." They wrote the piece to educate their readers about what transphobia is and why it matters. They claim that it should not be the responsibility of trans students to stop this form of oppression. They draw from their own experience as a trans college student and use data from interviews within their community at the university, quotes from trans students' Twitter feeds, and statistics about trans college students and youth.

Assignment Details

The op-ed lends itself to students selecting topics that impact their lives and communities. Too often, adolescents and young adults receive messages that they have to wait until they are adults to express identity-related concerns. However, our students have incredible expertise and insight that we can tap to help guide their advocacy and writing growth. You may invite students to think about issues connected to their local communities, interests, hobbies, or their already-in-place activism work (see Sample Op-Ed Assignment). Others need more guidance and support. You can ask students to find topics they care about, or you may want to choose a broad topic that is timely and relevant in the community that you know they can become invested in once they have the proper channels to filter their work. There are myriad ways to guide students towards a topic. Here are some:

- Tie topics to themes present in our classroom literature.
  - *The Iliad* and *The Odyssey* are canonical texts that lend themselves to themes associated with race, misogyny, and rights within the military.
- Watch the news and pick out interesting highlights.
  - Immigration is a highly charged and ever-present topic that impacts our state, schools, and students in Arizona. This is a topic I have asked high school and college students to reflect on, learn about, and argue a position for the writing of the op-ed because it has been at the heart of our conversations, reading, and current events.
- Turn to other subjects that they are actively engaged in.
  - A sixth-grade teacher in Phoenix I work with has her students write op-ed pieces about animal protection and conservation. This is a topic that younger students (and much older, too) love, and some organizations that do this work want to hear from youth voices.

One of the things I love about this genre, and one of the reasons it works so well with grades 6–12 and beyond, is that it pairs with the writing standards (as do all the genres in this book) and argument and research writing, yet the research is not overwhelming. In fact, this is a prime genre to teach students to scaffold or build toward a more comprehensive research project or paper. The op-ed gives them practice seeking and drawing from external sources, but without the length of a formal essay. Students may keep their opinion short, from 800–1200 words, to keep their audience engaged and fit the genre and publishing expectation. The op-ed takes 8–10 class sessions as a stand-alone writing unit. I have included a piece by a ninth-grader about the importance of funding public libraries, based on her own experience as a reader and library lover mentioned above (see Student Op-Ed Example).

Reading Connection

Teaching this genre with examples from that week's newspaper shows students how it is working in real-time in their communities. Providing examples from local community sources (e.g., city or college paper), state sources (e.g., state paper), and national or international sources (e.g., *New York Times* or *The Guardian*) facilitates a broad spectrum of models. Students may see how the same topic can be written about from different perspectives using different writing styles. Students can also visualize how these pieces change depending on the audience. Having students read three or four pieces connected to the same topic allows them see the repeated moves writers make in this genre. The goal is to support students in standing apart with voice and style when they write their op-ed. Leading students to annotate the model texts to find the critical genre elements is a strategy that helps with this genre and most others. Students can highlight the thesis, underline the counterclaim, and circle the evidence. Guide them to carefully read the lead and the conclusion and think about the author's writing moves to grab the reader's attention and make a call to action or sway the reader's opinion. Students may do this individually or collaboratively in small groups. Students should summarize the main idea or identify the writer's thesis or claim in this close reading exercise. Note: This is not always easy for students to find, and they may need support while doing this activity (see Sample Op-Ed Close Reading Activity with Sample Model Texts).

Here is an example of a collection of op-ed pieces I have used as model texts all connected to the topic of gender-neutral restrooms.

1. **University Paper:** (*The State Press*): Opinion: Gender-neutral restrooms deserve extra care
2. **State Paper:** (*Arizona Central*) My Turn: My transgender daughter was forced to leave her school
3. **National Paper:** (*LA Times*) Op-Ed: Everyone poops. No one should be stigmatized or criminalized when they answer nature's call
4. **International Paper:** (*The Guardian*) To those who oppose gender-neutral toilets: They're better for everybody

Along with a focused close reading of op-ed essays connected to one topic, it is useful to give students access to a variety of model texts. There are also resources for students to turn to for advice on how to write op-eds. For example, the *New York Times* has an article, "Tips for Aspiring Op-Ed Writers," and The OpEd Project has resources for learning to navigate this genre. Give these as readings for homework, read together as a class, and create a chart in the classroom with advice and tips for the genre. Or have them available for when students get stuck and need extra help. Giving students resources and tools to learn about and practice new genres helps demystify how writing works globally.

Writing Workshop Tip: Navigating Different Viewpoints

One of the things that we want students to understand in forming arguments is the power of laying competing claims side by side to acknowledge, honor, and respond to different perspectives. The op-ed article is a perfect genre to offer students some tools to practice this in their writing. Complement this at the prewriting and drafting stage by asking students to respond to the following questions, which require that they gather information to reflect on and acknowledge different perspectives to position themselves and make their case:

1. Why do I care about this issue? Why is it relevant to me?
2. Why is the issue relevant to others?
3. What event, research, or concern makes me want to get involved?
4. What has been an obstacle or reason I have not acted on this issue in the past? What could keep others from acting?
5. How can information or data help support my opinion?
6. What information or data help support an opposing viewpoint on this issue?
7. How do I want to influence this conversation?
8. What does the reader need to know to understand the issue, see it differently, or act?
9. Who must act? How?

Digital Tools

There are digital tools to support students in understanding media bias when considering balancing different opinions in their op-ed pieces. For example, AllSides is a site that focuses on media bias and shows top news stories from varying perspectives. It also rates news articles for bias. Students go to this space to see how one topic appears through different lenses. AllSides posts a "Story of the Week" headline news article that received a great deal of attention, with quotes from reporters representing all different perspectives from articles about the same topic. Students take part in argument mapping to think about their claim and back it up with evidence effectively and sequentially. Canva is a powerful tool that allows students to turn their pieces into newspaper-like articles complete with visual images and bylines. Students go wild over the images and format options.

Extensions

A natural extension of op-ed writing is to have students send their pieces out for publication or publish the pieces for the class or school more informally. Requiring students to send their work to formal venues for publication may not be safe, depending on immigration status or family support. In addition, students may not want their writing out in public for all eyes to see. Find ways for students to make their work public, but in ways that feel comfortable. Give students the resources they need to send to local papers and other publication venues by choice. The OpEd Project has a list of the country's top online and print publications. Although the list is not exhaustive, it is comprehensive and frequently updated. Many publications are open to op-ed and freelance submissions and writers of all ages. There are also calls for op-ed submissions for venues specific to teen writers, including Teen Ink and the *New York Times* Annual Student Editorial Contest. If students are writing about topics that connect to state, local, or national politics, they may want to contact their local representatives. For those students who do not want to write their representatives, show them alternatives, to help them to contact other key lawmakers:

- https://www.house.gov/leadership

If students are not ready or comfortable publishing their work formally, also create informal publishing opportunities within the confines of the classroom using a class newsletter or a class opinion blog.

MODEL TEXTS FOR OP-EDS

1. Song, I. (2014). Why more adults need to value teen voices. *Huffington Post.* https://www.huffpost.com/entry/teenager-misconceptions_b_5024803

2. Homayoun, A. (2018). What teens wish their parents knew about social media. *Washington Post.* https://www.washingtonpost.com/news/parenting/wp/2018/01/09/what-teens-wish-their-parents-knew-about-social-media/

3. Anina, N. (2021). Should young people be forced to get the Covid-19 vaccine? *The Teen Mag.* https://www.theteenmagazine.com/should-young-people-be-forced-to-get-the-covid-19-vaccine

4. Adams, J. (2019). My high school students don't read anymore and I think I know why. *Los Angeles Times.* https://www.latimes.com/opinion/story/2019-08-22/death-of-reading-high-school-cellphone

5. Abhayawickrama, N. (2021). Climate activism isn't making young people anxious. Climate change is." *The Guardian.* https://www.theguardian.com/commentisfree/2021/sep/04/climate-activism-isnt-making-young-people-anxious-climate-change-is

6. Carroll, A. E. (2020). The coronavirus has made it obvious. Teenagers should start school later," *New York Times.* https://www.nytimes.com/2020/05/27/opinion/coronavirus-teenagers-school-sleep.html

SAMPLE OP-ED ASSIGNMENT 1: PRACTICE CLOSE READING OF OP-ED PIECES

In this close reading exercise, the class will analyze three op-eds from a variety of sources to see examples of how they are constructed. Students will be reminded that the op-eds published in the newspaper will not always follow the conventions of academic writing students often use for formal essays, but the op-eds will contain a thesis (stated or implied), main points, and supporting evidence. They can also contain story and first-person experience and appeals to emotion.

Choose three of the op-eds from the list below to analyze as a group. Each group will share out using the below list as a guide.

1. Lead
2. Source
3. Main idea or thesis
4. Favorite quote from the piece and why
5. A sentence the piece does effectively

Op-Eds:

- Bettelheim, R. (2011). Gabrielle Giffords and you: The truth about brain injuries. *Huffington Post.* https://www.huffpost.com/entry/post_2120_b_877418
- Room, R. (2011). I hated the three-day breast cancer walk. *Huffington Post.* https://www.huffpost.com/entry/breast-cancer-walk_b_875664
- Ahmed, Q. A. (2011). Saudi ban on women driving is against Islam." *Christian Science Monitor.* https://www.csmonitor.com/Commentary/Opinion/2011/0617/Saudi-ban-on-women-driving-is-against-Islam
- Kielberger, C., & Keilberger, M. (2018). Dads deserve to be held to the same high standard as moms. *Huffington Post.* https://www.huffpost.com/archive/ca/entry/fathers-equal-responsibility-coparenting_a_23453470

SAMPLE OP-ED ASSIGNMENT 2:
WRITE TO CHANGE THE WORLD

Purpose: An op-ed is a piece of evidence-based argumentative writing that is timely and of public value. It also provides a platform to communicate your ideas to a broader audience with the intention of making a strong claim or suggestion. Op-eds are commonly published in newspapers and online sources and serve to sway public opinion and change minds using convincing argument and presenting it in a concise, readable way.

This assignment also provides you an opportunity to reflect on the writing process and to refamiliarize yourself with the conventions of engaged professional writing. This assignment is designed to teach you how to effectively use evidence in support of your argument and use precise language to emphasize important points.

Instructions: Compose a formal op-ed piece in response to an issue that you care about—a response you want to see in print. Take seriously the challenge of adding something new to the public conversation, something you would like to have people read. Take a position on any political, educational, or cultural issue.

Some questions that are useful to ask yourself when getting started:

- What specific issue or controversy are you responding to?
- Why is it important to consider this issue now?
- What evidence or insight have other authors offered in support of their position(s)?
- What is problematic about the claim and/or the evidence that other author(s) used?
- What additional evidence or insight do you have that could shed new light onto the matter at hand?

Lead

The first line of an op-ed is crucial. The leading sentence may grab the reader's attention with a strong claim, a surprising fact, a metaphor, a mystery, or a counterintuitive observation that entices the reader into reading more. The opening also briefly lays the foundation for your argument.

A news hook is what makes your piece timely and often is part of the lead. Be bold, but incontrovertible. Tell an anecdote if it illustrates your point. Use humor, if appropriate. Use clear sentences. Look at the leads we have analyzed in class.

Conclusions

Every good column or op-ed piece needs a strong ending that fulfills some basic requirements:

- Echoes or answers the introduction
- Has been foreshadowed by preceding thematic statements
- Is the last and often most memorable detail
- Contains a final epiphany or calls the reader to action

There are two basic types of endings. An open ending suggests rather than states a conclusion, while a closed ending states rather than suggests a conclusion. The closed ending in which the point of the piece is resolved is by far the most used.

Overall Format

Op-ed pieces run approximately 800–1200 words (at least four pages). Make sure to adhere to this convention. Do not exceed the word count; get used to writing succinctly. Writing less means you must be very precise. Your language should be professional and polished and free of grammatical and syntactical errors.

Please include: (1) a title and an acknowledgement of your target audience (potential publication outlet), (2) a conclusion with a one-sentence byline identifying yourself and your expertise (don't include title and byline in word count), and (3) an inspirational op-ed piece.

- Attach to your op-ed a copy of an editorial you admire from your desired publication. Mentally annotate that editorial, looking for such aspects

CONTINUED

as an opening hook, placement of thesis statement, length of sentences, and the closing punch line. This inspirational piece should come from the type of publication in which you would most like to see your op-ed piece in print.

- Research also allows a reader to include sensory data (touch, taste, smell, sound, or sight) into a column. There are two basic methods of research:
  - Field research: going to the scene, interviews, legwork; primary materials, observations, and knowledge
  - Library, academic, or internet research: using secondary materials, including graphs, charts, and scholarly articles
- Consider the intended audience of the publication and the way in which your op-ed reaches that demographic. If possible, look up the submission guidelines at the journal or newspaper or editorial service where you will submit your writing. I will compare the stylistics of the published example to your own op-ed when I grade your work.

Due Dates

- Proposal: About a half page with the topic of your op-ed and title of your op-ed inspirational piece explaining why you chose this topic due _____.
- First 500 words and op-ed inspiration piece for in-class peer-review due _____.
- Rough draft due _____.
- Peer review due _____.
- Final draft due _____.

Evaluation Criteria

Your op-ed will be evaluated according to the following criteria. You may find it helpful to revisit these questions throughout your writing process. Each question constitutes 10 possible points:

1. Is the writing style appropriate for the target audience?
2. Does the writer take a position? Indicate where in the essay you found this statement.

3. Is the claim contestable (i.e., is there more than one way to look at the issue)?

4. Does the writer account for the contestability of the issue?

5. Does the writer make a strong argument? (Hint: Could you easily outline the main points?)

6. Is the argument logical? Is it well organized? Is it clear?

7. Does the writer provide you with enough information so that you could review the evidence for yourself (if you were so inclined)?

8. Is the writer's reasoning logically sound?

9. Does the author provide an engaging hook at the beginning of the essay that would be appropriate and interesting for their target audience? Or an audience that may not already have interest in the topic?

10. Note the specific aspects of the essay that seemed most engaging to you and explain why.

11. Can you underline a sentence (or two) that indicates precisely what the author wants readers to do with the information in this essay (i.e., is there a call to action)?

12. Do you have any specific questions or suggestions about how the writer might develop, extend, qualify, make more precise, complicate, or rethink the essay's central point and supporting evidence? If so, please offer them here.

Publishing Your Op-Ed

Although it is not required for the course, I encourage you to submit your polished op-ed for publication.

Sample Assigment Source: Andrea Rivers, community college composition instructor

Ninth-Grade Student

Keep Libraries Open

I ride my bike to the library every Saturday with my dad. We always stop and get hot cocoa (for me) and coffee (for my dad) and then head to the corner of Rural and Southern and wait for the light to change so we can cross safely. Once we cross the busy street and lock our bikes and helmets at the bike racks in front of the library, we walk down the sidewalk entry past the people asking for signatures for the latest ballot measures. We walk up to the door. But this past week when we tried to open the front doors, they were locked. The library had changed its hours. It is no longer open all day on Saturdays, which is the only day my dad is not working, and I am not in school.

My dad said, "We can drop off our books and then come back next week and we won't have any fines." But the book drop was closed too. We returned home on our bikes feeling frustrated with our-soon-to-be overdue books. As I pedaled home, I kept thinking about why the library was closed in the afternoons now and I asked my dad. He said it is a lack of funding and that libraries don't have the money they need to stay open as often. I started to think about ways I could help bring funding back to public libraries that I love so much. I believe libraries should be open all the time—24 hours a day. People should always have a place to go to feel safe and a place to go to find and read a book.

I remember going to the library every Saturday when I was little to storytime downstairs in the children's section. We sat on big pillows and listened to the librarian read books with her magic voice. I remember playing hide and seek in between the bookshelves and making bookmarks at the art table. I remember finding my first chapter books that were graphic novels about a boy spy detective. I found it at the library in the children's section and after finding one, went on to read the whole series. After that, I found Kate DiCamillo's books. I started with *Because of Winn Dixie* and read every book I could find of hers that the library had.

Without public libraries, I would not have found these memories or these books. I would not have had those afternoons with my dad. I remember when the library got new computer scanners to check out books and my dad let me scan my stack to check out. I love the sound of the beep every time I put the barcode over the scanner. We are allowed to check out as many books as we want. My dad says I can check out as many as will fit in my bike basket or backpack. Sometimes, in the middle of the summer when the heat in the desert is too intense for us to ride bikes, my dad will drive us, and we will spend extra time in the cool air conditioning of the library. I want to be a librarian one day. I want to help people find books and organize them on the shelves.

I have been to the library so often to find books, to get answers or help with school projects and to answer questions. Now, as my library is closing its doors because of a lack of support, I want to help. We need to find ways to support libraries so they cannot just have their regular hours but stay open day and night. Libraries are an important safe space for everyone. We need money to hire librarians and to support these wonderful sanctuaries in our cities. Libraries need new books and computers and supplies. I plan to send a letter to the mayor and my congresswoman and senators about this issue. I hope that you will do whatever you can to help support your public library so that our libraries can stay open and other young and old readers will fall in love with books pulled from the library's shelves.

CHAPTER 6

The Profile

Profile essays are a pervasive form of nonfiction writing that tell the story of everyday and extraordinary individuals. David Remnick, the editor of *The New Yorker,* describes the profile as ". . . a biographical piece—a concise rendering of a life through anecdote, incident, interview, and description (or some ineffable combination thereof)" (Rothman, 2012). However, writing fitting Remnick's definition of the profile appeared in newspapers and magazines years prior; a staff writer for *The New Yorker* was the first to coin the term "profile" to describe a journalistic biographical sketch. The profile became a particular feature of *The New Yorker* and is now widely found in various analog and digital text and media forms.

The *New York Times* features a Saturday profile essay of "individuals shaping the world around them" (2022). The recurring column profiles athletes, graduate students, priests, actors, environmental activists, and politicians. *Sports Illustrated* has a website called Fan Nation, an offshoot of its print magazine, and it recently published a column called "Player Profile" to share the stories of individual athletes. *Time Magazine* features a profile in almost every issue and is famous for its profile highlighting "The Time Magazine Person of the Year." The blog *Humans of New York* has published thousands of everyday people from New York City. The blog began as a series of photographs of New Yorkers and then morphed into short profile pieces with interviews and pictures. On the blog's About tab, Brian Stanton states, "HONY now has over twenty million followers on social media and provides a worldwide audience with daily glimpses into the lives of strangers on the streets of New York City" (HONY, n.d.). The profile serves as an informative text in each space, working as a window into human experience.

Writing in-depth profile essays and going through the writing process from the invention, drafting, interviewing, internet research, peer review, and revision to final sharing typically takes four to five weeks with 2–3 days a week of instructional focus. If this timing is not feasible, you are working with younger writers, or you have other longer essays assignments and want to break things up, you can have students write profile snapshots instead of in-depth essays. The profile snapshot has the exact genre expectations of a profile essay but is condensed. It serves as a glimpse of a detailed experience, so the snapshots highlight speakers for a series. For example, my department at the university has a speaker series every semester featuring prominent authors. These events are each advertised with brief snapshots of the speakers along with the event details (e.g., date, time, zoom link, RSVP). Profile snapshots can be found in pamphlets, promotional materials, news articles, and blogs (e.g., *Humans of New York*).

Regardless of snapshot or longer essay form, the profile's focus is up to you and your students. Profiles typically describe a person or group from a particular angle. The profile typically involves primary (interviewing) and secondary (internet) research. The profile writer takes a stance or angle on that person they are profiling and describes them as something. Then the writer tries to convince the reader of the validity of that perspective. For instance, a writer might profile a student activist within their school or community as an example of a successful adolescent student and changemaker. Academic record and strong work ethic are two components worth mentioning. Teaching students to take an angle for their profiles and reading examples is essential to understanding this genre.

As a focus for the profile genre, you can invite students to focus on changemakers from their communities, people in careers they are interested in pursuing, or living authors students read and admire. This last option is an author profile, which generally shares an author's background, such as where they grew up and who their influences were, what they have published, and what works they are mainly known for. Profile pieces usually take an angle or stance to help focus the writing. If, for example, a famous YA literature author has typically written coming-of-age nonfiction pieces and has a new work that is an entirely different genre, the profile writer could approach the profile with the angle that the author is breaking out of their comfort zone and stepping into uncharted territory. On the other hand, if the author is part of a larger movement of writers, the angle could be to focus on that movement and how that author fits into it and why.

Interviews offer students the chance to learn from the people they profile through structured dialogue and careful listening. Student interviews allow students to connect with relevant people and create investment in the project by providing choices regarding the person. When I taught a year-long, ninth-grade curriculum related to activism, students interviewed people doing activism work that interested them and they wanted to learn more about (Early, 2006). I gave them the freedom to connect with people they already knew and admired or find new people. Students interviewed people like counselors, physicians, local environmental activists, voting rights advocates, surfers working on protecting oceans, and urban planners working to create more green spaces.

Similarly, when I taught 12th grade, I asked students to write profiles of individuals who shared a passion or an interest. Ronaldo interviewed his martial arts instructor. Blake chose a musician who is a member of a local band he admires. Chrissie reconnected with her middle school volleyball coach. These young people discovered local mentors. Several students chose to interview members of their families. Cecilia interviewed her grandfather when he was visiting from Guatemala. Dhyana interviewed her father and gained new insights into his life as he told her about fleeing Tibet. The profile assignment provides a way for students to learn more about their families and communities and gain new respect for and insights into their culture, roots, or life interests and goals. It is impressive to see our students' intelligence, depth, and good-heartedness through whom they choose to interview and profile. The interview and profile write-up are genuinely an exchange. Profiles build a bridge from the classroom to the community.

You can help make these connections for students through your contacts or cold calling or emailing people in the community. While involving some effort, it is well worth giving every student access. If students are profiling authors, you can have them reach out to the authors via email—even famous ones. You will be surprised how many respond. When my daughter was in sixth grade, she wrote to Lemony Snicket (pen name), the author of *A Series of Unfortunate Events,* because she was dying to ask him a question about a character. She received an email back from his agent and then two days later from the author himself. This is a tangible way for students to connect to people they admire and to realize they are not as distant or inaccessible as they may seem. If authors don't respond, students may rely on information gathered from other sources and materials to create a dynamic and engaging profile of an author they admire.

To help students gain familiarity with the profile in either the snapshot or essay form, you can give them time to read model texts and conduct a genre analysis. The model texts should reflect the work you want them to produce. For example, if you want them to write profile snapshots, then have models of snapshots. If you wish to enact a profile essay, provide essay examples. The genre analysis represents a way for students to read the collection of pieces to understand how the genre works and the moves writers make across texts and within the genre form.

Genre Analysis Guiding Questions

1. Who is the audience?
2. In what context is this genre often used?
3. Who typically uses this genre and for what purpose?
4. How is this genre formatted (e.g., paragraphs, lists, greetings)?
5. What are any visual cues that are important (e.g., bullets, highlights, bolding)?
6. What is the level of formality in the language?
7. What kind of information does the author tell about the person they are profiling (e.g., facts, quotes, references, images)?

See the Model Texts section at the end of this chapter for examples of profile snapshots and essays focused on individuals working toward positive change. There are also examples of author profiles. They may be used as model texts or simply serve as examples of the kind of collection of texts you can gather to create a text set of your own to match the profile topic you want your students to pursue.

Assignment Details

The guidelines for the profile assignment are straightforward. Students write about a person they may or may not know personally but want to know better for a reason you help clarify. For the profile essay contents, you can ask students to introduce the person they have interviewed, share the person's significant life and career pathways, and share what they, as the writer, learned through the experience of interviewing or researching this individual. You want to make clear to students that they should choose an angle or focus for the piece. They can think about this question to help find an angle: What is the central aspect of this person's life or work that they want to emphasize and why? It is also helpful to give students tips to guide their understanding and writing of this genre:

Tips for Writing Profiles

- A profile creates a picture through the selective use of detail. Every anecdote, quote, and descriptive fact must contribute in a meaningful way toward your primary impression of the person.
- A profile typically uses the present tense to create a sense of relevance and closeness for the readers. You make a more effective relationship between the audience and your profile subject when you help them feel a part of the people and events you describe.
- While focusing on a particular person and their experiences, a writer can draw attention to the larger social implications of that person's life. Every person's story is embedded in a larger social context and is connected to the beliefs and experiences of others. Your purpose could be to draw a more significant meaning from a particular profile. How is this person's story relevant to others and you?
- Although focused mainly on the story of a single person, this writing and information about who they are and what they have achieved or learned becomes a way for you to reflect on your own life, interests, and perspective.
- If the profile subject is a family member or a friend, or at least not a famous person, the student should obtain the subject's permission to be profiled in the project. If the student cannot get permission, the student should disguise the subject's identity as much as possible (see the Author's Note on privacy).

- You also want to let your interviewees know you are profiling them for a class project and ask for their verbal permission.

During the weeks we focus on profile writing, students study the qualities of a strong profile essay. They carefully follow the writing process, complete a detailed outline as part of the prewriting and planning activity, and submit their rough draft to their writers' groups (three to four students) for peer review.

Manageable Steps to Break Down the Teaching of This Genre
1. Brainstorm and choose a person to profile. Have a Plan A and B.
2. Contact the person via email to ask for an interview.
3. Write an interview protocol with 8–10 questions.
4. Interview the person either in person, via Zoom, or by email.
5. Research the issue, topic, or organization the person works on or with. This can take place in class online or in the library.
6. Write the profile and revise.
7. Share with peers, teachers, and the people interviewed.

One of my first-year college students, John, wrote a profile essay about a transgender activist who hugely impacted John's life as a high school student. In this essay, John shares how he befriended Zoey, the transgender activist. He describes the way she has influenced change on a local level through the LGBT community. In the middle part of the essay, John shares how Zoey called him out for his beliefs and helped him view gender and sexuality differently and in ways that made a lasting impact on his confidence and commitment in pursuit of LGBTQ acceptance and rights. John wrote this profile for my first-year college Early Start program at the university. The assignment was to profile a person in the world doing work to influence positive change.

In a high school class working on profile snapshots of changemakers, Aja, a 10th-grader, wrote hers about a psychologist she had interviewed because she admires the way psychologists make a positive difference in people's mental well-being. Aja wanted to interview and learn about this person's work to understand a career path she hopes to pursue one day. Aja's profile snapshot teaches others about the work of a remarkable scientist, Isabel Q., and shares a sincere connection to Isabel's work. Through Aja's access to, interview with, and write-up of an interview with a woman scientist, Aja began to form her understanding of what it means to be a woman in science and, more specifically, a psychologist. The profile snapshot reminds me how learning about other people's life stories provides opportunities to envision and try on new ways of thinking about and acting in the world. (Both essays are in the Student Examples at the end of this chapter.)

Reading Connection

Writing a profile lends itself to having students read books of choice. The books can be connected to some aspect of the person they are profiling. For example, if they (or you) choose to profile people working toward positive social change, they can read a nonfiction book about the kind of activism work or issue. If students profile people with a shared passion or interest, they can read any genre connected to that interest. For example, one of my former 12th-grade students working on a person's profile in a career he hoped to pursue one day chose to profile a comic artist in the community. For his book of choice, he selected *Reinventing Comics* by Scott McLoud (2000), which provided him with a rich history of the comic industry and one comic artist's journey within it. Another one of my students, who is legally blind, chose to profile a teacher of the blind at a local school. For her book of choice, she read Helen Keller's *The Miracle Worker* (1984). Nate, a passionate skateboarder, chose to profile an owner of a skate shop in town because he hopes to pursue a career connected to skateboarding. He was amazed to find an autobiography of his hero, Tony Hawk, to read for his book of choice.

Book choice is crucial in creating a balance between freedom and structure for students within a language arts curriculum. Students need a basic design to serve as a foundation for their learning. A strong curriculum provides a launching pad to expand students' conversations about issues that matter in their lives and futures. To match the reading abilities and individual interests of a diverse student population, you may offer opportunities like these to choose from a wide array of texts revolving around a specific topic and connected to the genre they are writing.

Students need to know how to read, question, reread, write, and talk about unfamiliar and challenging texts that they or others select for them.

These skills prepare students for the higher education and the workplace and their lives as readers. Students may learn all the necessary reading skills, and you can cover all the needed standards for teaching reading while reading books they choose. You can give them time in class to read and respond to their texts to assess their understanding and progress. You can privilege the practice of reading within your classroom. One way to do this in the early stages is to have students write first impressions of their books; as they read, they can write timelines to track the events of their books. They can also keep a log to track their questions and impressions. When students complete their books of choice, you can have them write reflections. Another option is a book hunt, when students spend a class period asking classmates about the books they have read and what they have learned from them.

BOOK CHOICE BOOK HUNT

1. Find someone whose book has a main character that makes an important change. What is the book? What is the change?
2. Find someone whose book deals with themes of racial justice. What is the book? What are the issues?
3. Find someone whose book deals with environmental issues. What is the book? What are the issues?
4. Find someone whose book honors working-class jobs or working-class life. What is the book? How is the work or the working class honored?
5. Find someone whose book deals with a conventional topic in an unconventional way. What's the book? How does it deal with the topic?
6. Find someone whose book has incredibly strong women characters. What is the book? How do women manifest their strength in the book?
7. Find someone whose book addresses hardship. What is this hardship, and how is it addressed in the book?
8. Find someone whose book is filled with hope. What is the book? What is it about the book that leaves readers hopeful?

The work surrounding book choice provides multiple opportunities to learn about and understand the work or lives of people out in the world who matter to students in diverse ways. The books of choice allow students to dive into stories about far-away people and make these people seem vibrant and real. Students learned how people like the Dalai Lama, Muhammad Ali, Julia Butterfly Hill, Nathan McCall, Gloria Steinem, and Tom McCall are connected to families, schools, neighborhoods, trauma, and hope. These books give students sophisticated and complex stories on which to practice honing their reading skills and to begin to think about issues and pathways that matter for their own lives.

Writing Workshop Tips:
Mini Lessons on Learning to Ask

Students often come to the profile project excited and nervous to connect with people doing work they admire out in the world. When they start interviewing people, they usually know who they want to connect with, but they often have trouble articulating why, other than in generalizations. Students need help thinking about the person they want to interview and why they want to interview them. It helps to take students through a process of asking themselves what they want to get out of this project and then practice writing an interview protocol and a formal email to ask for an interview. To brainstorm areas of interest in connection to the profile assignment and the person they plan to interview, you can have students write a brief "First Thoughts Note" sharing answers to question such as:

1. Who do you want to interview and why?
2. How is this person connected to a life path or work in the world you can see yourself pursuing?
3. What do you want to know about this person if you only have a few minutes with them and why?
4. What questions do you have or help do you need?

Using writing to articulate and brainstorm ideas allows students to clarify their thinking and solidify their plans. This note format offers a different way for students to experience schooled writing as informal and needs based. Students may express interest, need, and a vision for their futures through note writing. In essence, the note format encourages students to ask for what they need in as specific a way as possible within a supportive classroom space and gives you information to guide them in their next steps.

Another form of asking, which is often new for students, is interviewing. Students need help learning how to create successful interview questions and form questions connected to what they want to know for their profiles. They need help thinking about how what they ask will directly correlate with the information they will gather. Although this seems obvious, it isn't to our students navigating a new social practice. Helping students to create an interview protocol, complete with 10–12 general information questions, is a strong start. This will include who the person is, why they care about an issue they are working on, how they became interested in the issue, what they do to make a change, why they think it matters, and what they hope others know about doing it differently. You can provide students with tips for creating their interview questions that encourage lively interviews.

Tips for Writing Interview Questions
1. Avoid yes or no questions.
2. Keep questions on the topic.
3. Ask questions that cannot be answered by doing research.
4. Invite the interviewee to share a story or example.
5. Write questions to encourage the interviewee to expand on ideas.
6. At the end, invite the interviewee to share something you did not ask that they might think is important for you to know.

The interviews give students a window into the diverse pathways individuals follow as they prepare for, enter, and participate in different kinds of work in the world. The profile essay gives students a chance to reach out individually to people they admire and want to learn more about within their communities. As students reach out and receive answers to their interviews, they compare their interview experiences with their peers. They share the stories of the individuals they interviewed, the obstacles they faced in the interview process, and ideas for their final profile pieces. As part of their interview profile essays, students reflect on the interview experience and the workshop. They emphasize how this writing project represents a new kind of learning, requiring them to reach beyond the classroom and out into the community, for example, to understand the intricate choices women make to become successful scientists. After students complete the writing of the main part of their profile piece, we ask them to reflect on what they learned through the experience of interviewing. You can ask students to write responses to the following questions to guide this reflective aspect of the profile essay:

1. Please take time to share what you learned in the process of writing your profile.
2. What did you notice about your writing process?
3. What did you learn about the person you studied that you will remember?

This lesson and related writing activities help students learn rhetorical skills and genre conventions, the ones typically used in interview questions and processes to gain knowledge about individuals out in the world. You also can cover both oral and written interviews in discussing interview questions since students may conduct email interviews.

Digital Tools

Digital tools enhance the research process for students as they gather the information they need to write profile pieces. They can use Evernote to take notes as they research the work, organization, or cause of the person they profile. If students conduct their interviews online, they can use Zoom or Google Meet, which are growing in popularity with writers and journalists for remote interviews. For in-person interviews, students may not realize it, but one of the best tools for recording audio interviews—even remotely—comes standard on their phone: the Voice Memo function. If students conduct their interviews via Zoom, they can record and set an audio-only version of the meeting to capture the transcript of the event to then use direct excerpts in the profile write-up. Both platforms offer free versions and allow students to record the video and audio of the interview.

You can also take the profile writing a step further and ask students to create a digital profile that tells the person's story using voice-over, images, and music to tell the story. Applications within Canva or Adobe Spark also aid students with creating digital profiles. An example is Sophie McAdam's digital profile of Elora Hardy, a sustainable architect working to establish bamboo as a material of choice in the construction industry (McAdam, 2014).

Extensions

At the core of this curriculum is the social nature of writing. Students choose topics based on their interests, friendships, hobbies, and relationships. They reach out to people to interview and learn from. Ultimately, they have an audience to write for and share. After students complete their profile essays or snapshots, you can take the time to share these as a community. You can do this in a circle in the classroom and have each student take the role of "Author's Chair." They come to the front of the room to read their piece aloud or share their digital recording. You can also invite students to send their profile pieces to the people they profiled to make their work public and honor the people who gave them time and attention. You can also create a physical or digital profile gallery in the classroom, a shared public space in the school (library or front office or bulletin board), or online (class blog or newsletter) to share the profiles with a wider audience. Most importantly, you can invite students to send their profile pieces out to the publication venues they selected early on as their audience for the piece.

MODEL TEXTS FOR THE PROFILE

Profile Snapshots

1. Profile: Judith Kitinga, Tanzanian gender activist: Africa Renewal, by Adam Melville. This article shares a brief profile of a young activist in Tanzania working toward gender equality https://www.sierraleonetimes .com/news/257906018/profile-judith-kitinga-tanzanian-gender-activist

1. 'Young people are angry': the teenage activists shaping our future, by Candice Pires, May 13, 2018. *The Guardian.* This article shares three profiles of teenage activists. Each profile represents a profile example. https://www.theguardian.com/society/2018/may/13/young-people- are-angry-meet-the-teenage-activists-shaping-our-future

2. I Want to Start from Scratch: How Teen Black Lives Matter Activists Are Writing the Future. *Elle Magazine.* This article profiles adolescents working toward racial justice. https://headtopics .com/us/i-want-to-start-from-scratch-how-teen-black-lives-matter -activists-are-writing-the-future-14509602

3. Parkland Students: Meet the Teens Leading the Gun Control Movement. *Business Insider.* This article profiles students who have become activists for gun control after the Parkland school shooting. https://www.busines sinsider.com/who-are-young-people-leading-march-for-our-lives -gun-control-movement-2018-3

Profile Essays

1. Becoming Greta: "Invisible Girl" to Global Climate Activist, With Bumps Along the Way, by Somini Sengupta, February 18, 2019. https://www. nytimes.com/2019/02/18/climate/greta-thunburg.html. This essay profiles Greta Thunberg who overcame crippling depression to become one of the world's most influential youth environmental activists.

2. These NYC teens center climate science in their activism—and their ambitious experiments. Now they'll compete on the world stage, by Amy Zimmer, April 21, 2021, *Chalkbeat.* https://ny.chalkbeat.org/2021/4/21/22396734/ climate-science-behruz-mahmudov-kayla-wang. This profile essay focuses on the work of two teen climate activists from Queens, New York. They paired their interest in science with a passion to support climate change and started studying plant adaptations and climate change.

MODEL TEXTS FOR THE PROFILE

3. Assa Traoré and France's Fight for Racial Justice. *Time Magazine.* https://time.com/5919814/guardians-of-the-year-2020-assa-traore/. This essay profile's a youth activist in France who works against police brutality after the death of her own brother and in connection to the #BlackLivesMatter Movement.

4. How Anthony Fauci Became America's Doctor by Michael Specter, April 10, 2020, *The New Yorker.* https://www.newyorker.com/magazine/2020/04/20/how-anthony-fauci-became-americas-doctor. This in-depth profile essay focuses on the career of Dr. Anthony Fauci who has become a leader in the United States and beyond during the COVID-19 pandemic.

5. Designer Builds Million-Dollar Bamboo Mansions in Bali: Photos, by Claire Turrell, June 14, 2021, *Insider.* https://www.insider.com/bamboo-mansions-bali-photos-elora-hardy-ibuku-feature-2021-$2 This essay profiles the life pathway and work of Elora Hardy, a former model turned environmental architect who has become a leader in designing buildings using bamboo in Bali.

6. The Awakening of Colin Kaepernick, by John Branch, September 7, 2017, *New York Times.* https://www.nytimes.com/2017/09/07/sports/colin-kaepernick-nfl-protests.html. This profile shares the life pathway of Colin Kaepernick to show how he became one of the most famous sports activists in history.

Author Profiles

1. Who Jason Reynolds Writes His Best-sellers For, by Rumaan Alam, August 9, 2021, *The New Yorker.* https://www.newyorker.com/magazine/2021/08/16/who-jason-reynolds-writes-his-best-sellers-for. This essay profiles the life pathway of Jason Reynolds, one of the most popular and award-winning young adult authors in the United States. Much of Reynold's writing draws on his own lived experience growing up in an all-Black community.

2. Caught Between Worlds? For Elizabeth Acevedo, It's a Familiar Feeling, by Concepción de León, May 4, 2020, *New York Times.* https://www.nytimes.com/2020/05/04/books/elizabeth-acevedo-clap-when-you-

CONTINUED

land-poet-x.html. This essay profiles the life and work of poet and writer, Elizabeth Acevedo. Acevedo is a Dominican American National Book Award winner and the first writer of color to win the Carnegie Medal. She has written *The Poet X* and *With the Fire on High*.

3. Tommy Orange and the New Native Renaissance, by *Julian Brave Noise-Cat*, June 29, 2018, *The Paris Review*. https://www.theparisreview.org/blog/2018/06/29/tommy-orange-and-the-new-native-renaissance/. This essay focuses on the work and life story of Tommy Orange, a Native American author from Oakland, California who is part of a new generation of Native writers.

4. A Profile of Children's Literature Legacy Award Winner Jacqueline Woodson, by Deborah Taylor, September 6, 2018, *Horn Book*. https://www.hbook.com/story/profile-childrens-literature-legacy-award-winner-jacqueline-woodson. Deborah Taylor profiles her good friend and famous author, Jacqueline Woodson. Woodson is a Children's and YA Literature author known for her books about young people and mostly, but not exclusively, about young African Americans.

SAMPLE PROFILE ESSAY ASSIGNMENT: CHANGEMAKER PROFILE ESSAY

Description of a Profile Essay: Your profile essay will be an intensive study of a person working toward positive social change related to an issue that matters deeply to you. You will examine this person's practices as an activist and changemaker within the context of their work or life. The goal is to use reading, writing, and research to learn as much as possible about this person and learn more about what it means to influence change in the world.

Process: Your case study will involve a person of your choice who influences change in connection to an issue that matters deeply to you.

This assignment invites you to do the following:

1. Learn about a changemaker of your choice from your community or lived experience. It should be someone you know or know of well. You will share their changemaking through your writing and examples from two or three texts (e.g., articles, books, chapters, news) or one to two observations, an interview (in person or email), informal conversations (in person or on the phone), emails, or connection points, photographs, or memories.
2. Identify the main goal or focus of the individual's work as a changemaker.
3. Select a strategy this person uses in their work as a changemaker and find a way to understand it profoundly. Explain this strategy in detail and provide examples. How could you implement the strategy on a micro level in your own life?
4. Reflect on what this individual's work offers others and what it offers you.
5. Share why this person is essential to you in your pathway into the future as a young adult.
6. This will involve a systematic investigation of one changemaker you admire profoundly or want to learn more about from your community, experience, or background.

Research

Regardless of whom you choose to profile, you should research the person thoroughly. If you have done a complete job researching the person or their work, you might not use all the information you find but you will better understand the person. Your primary research should be an interview. This research technique allows you to add more personal and original elements to your profile. You may also need to complete some archival research (library or web-based research) to better understand the person, the person's career, or the person's interests.

Audience

You must begin to understand how necessary it is to have a specific audience when writing beyond your peers and me (the teacher). Making decisions about your writing always depends on knowing whom you're writing for and why you're writing. For this assignment, choose a publication venue for your profile and write for that venue. This venue needs to be appropriate for the person you are profiling and why you're profiling them. For example, you could profile a person in your neighborhood or community and publish it in the community newsletter (after studying the conventions of the newsletter's profiles and their publication guidelines). Attach a description of your publication venue to both your rough and final drafts of your profile.

Length

The length of your paper will vary depending on your publication venue, but for most platforms, your paper should be at least three pages long (double-spaced)—about 750 words. Please use a 12-point font. If graphics are allowable and appropriate for your publication venue, you may include a graphic (e.g., image, graph, table) that visually highlights some aspect of your profile. If your visual shares important details and conveys your piece's main idea or angle, the text itself might be as short as 500 words.

| | SAMPLE PROFILE ESSAY ASSIGNMENT *CONTINUED* | |

Assessment Criteria

I will consider the following criteria as I read your paper:

- The profile should create a strong impression of the person, using meaningful detail.
- The profile should address the intended audience and be appropriate for your chosen publication venue.
- The organization should be easy to follow and contribute to creating the dominant impression. The introduction should catch the reader's attention, and the conclusion should provide a reflection on how you are influenced by this person or by the process of writing the profile.
- The profile should effectively incorporate research from a firsthand interview you conducted. If you use library sources, the material should not dominate the paper; the material should simply contribute details to the dominant impression. Sources should be cited in MLA format.
- Overall, the profile should be clear and free of errors.

Due Dates

Bring one electronic copy of your rough draft to class on _____ so you can participate in the peer review workshop. When you submit your final draft on _____ , please attach your rough draft(s) and other materials you used while writing your paper. Also, remember to attach a description of your publication venue (name, organization, or company sponsoring the publication, intended audience, size of circulation, frequency of publication if a periodical) to all drafts. If you have any questions or concerns about the profile assignment, please contact me.

PROFILE ESSAY STUDENT EXAMPLE 1

First-Year College Student

La Mujer Fuerte

Estrella is a transgender activist who lives in the small town in California where I grew up. She has been a part of the LGBTQ movement since she first came out at the age of nine. Before I met Estrella my sophomore year of high school, I was not very aware of much that was happening in the LGBTQ community. This type of ignorance was precisely the thing she targeted to stop. I would have been a totally different person if it wasn't for her. I would have been uncomfortable in my own skin.

Before I met Estrella, I had just moved to my small town from a big city. When I started my new school, Estrella was the talk of the school because she had just released a new documentary that followed her path to womanhood. In the film she was given the opportunity to have her own Quince by her godmothers. They wanted Estrella to finally feel like a real woman. The documentary was well received by viewers. She had rented out our local theatre to introduce the documentary to a larger audience.

My first interaction with Estrella was during an anti-Trump protest before the 2016 presidential election. This event was a school-wide walkout where we left during lunch and did not return until classes had ended. During the walkout, we walked for two and a half hours all over our town, which led us into the neighboring towns as well. Estrella was one of the lead student speakers at the event and she kept us eager and energetic as we endured the summer heat. I had walked alongside Estrella because I was new at the school and wanted to make friends.

Our friendship was not an immediate one. She, along with many of the social justice warriors at the school did not like me because I was from Arizona. They thought I would have political views that did not match their own. I also kept my sexuality to myself because I had internalized the homophobia I had experienced before my move. Many of the comments I made may have seemed homophobic at that time because that was my sense of humor and what I had known growing up. Estrella, however, did not let me get away with this kind of humor. She immediately told me to stop and explained why I was being hurtful.

PROFILE ESSAY STUDENT EXAMPLE 1 *CONTINUED*

At the time, I did not know about her transition from male to female. When I told her about my own sexuality, her view of me completely changed. She was really upset that I was bisexual and homophobic. No one had ever called me out before for saying hateful things and I had never been around people who stopped this behavior or saw it as wrong. Estrella took me on as her project. She educated me on LGBTQ issues.

This allowed me to get close to her and to learn more about her childhood. Estrella came out at the age of nine right after her father had passed away. During this time, for about a year or two, she experienced abuse in her family. She kept things quiet until she was 14, when she told her mother. "I couldn't stand my mother because I opened up about the abuse I had experienced, and she told me I was trying to get attention." Estrella lived from then on without trusting her family to support her.

Estrella left home when she was 17 and continued her education at a continuation school. She was determined and began working to support herself. As I caught up with Estrella for this profile essay, she revealed to me how many times she was ready to quit everything. She continued to persevere because she did not want to be another statistic of trans people who die from lack of family support. "It was so messed up because I had to constantly act like I had the best mom ever and I really resented her for not being the mother she presented herself as to the world." Estrella wants to be known as someone who overcame struggle and transphobia to become a thriving student, activist, and woman.

I asked Estrella's permission to write this piece. She told me she hopes her story helps others. She has made such a difference to people within our community and has educated those, like me, who were not fortunate enough to know what LGBTQ rights really are. After many of her friends left her while she followed her own path, she continued her political movement with the help of her boyfriend and his family. "I think a great message I'd like to get out there is that despite my struggle, I had the ability to stay here and stick it out." Estrella helped changed the way I see other people and how I see myself. She taught me to be more accepting, to understand what it means to be comfortable in your own skin, and to fight for the rights of others.

PROFILE ESSAY STUDENT EXAMPLE 2

Tenth-Grade Student

Everything Is There for a Reason

Isabel Q. faced many problems in her path to becoming a psychologist. Among these problems was being away from her family and facing the fear of being alone. The school she attended was far from where she lived, and she had financial problems, such as paying for her education, housing, and personal needs. Although she faced these obstacles, nothing stopped her passion for helping others.

Isabel is a psychologist. She is interested in other people's behavior and why they act the ways they do. Her interests moved on to helping people to overcome their problems and grow even better as people. She wants to help people learn to be happy with themselves. She says, "It gives me a great feeling seeing people better than how they were the first time." Psychologists are people who listen to you. They help you overcome your problems and face difficult situations.

Like most people, Isabel has second-guessed her career. "If I had the opportunity to change my career, I would choose medicine," she said. Her biggest fear as a psychologist is not being able to help one of her patients. Her goal is to help people face their problems and change their attitudes about obstacles they face.

From this interview experience, I take away the feeling that helping others is the best thing to do consistently. You never know if you are the only person helping someone else. In the end, you might help them to feel happier or to live better with themselves. This is one of my future goals. I was once there for someone who was contemplating suicide. This was the first time I realized that helping people is what I want to do. The person I helped had many problems, but she told me I helped by being there for her. This interview made me grow as a person, and my passion for my future career as a psychologist increased.

References

Early, J. S. (2006). *Stirring up justice: Writing and reading to change the world.* Portsmouth, NH: Heinemann.

McAdam, S. (2014). "Meet the woman building stunning sustainable homes from bamboo," *True Activist.* https://www.trueactivist.com/breathtakingly -beautiful-bamboo-homes-in-bali-t1/

Statton, B. (2021). Humans of New York, https://www.humansofnewyork.com

New York Times. (2022). The Saturday Profile, https://www.nytimes.com/ column/the-saturday-profile

CHAPTER 7

The Podcast

L istening to podcasts is now a worldwide practice, and the popularity of this genre is only growing. People are plugging their earbuds or headphones in and listening to stories covering a range of interests including comedy, therapy, self-help, politics, sports, cooking, and current affairs. At the time I am writing this, there are 2 million podcasts and 48 million episodes available, and these numbers are climbing (Winn, 2021). According to Nielson ratings, over 50% of homes in the US listen to podcasts, and people who follow podcasts typically listen to seven shows per week (PPL PRS, 2021; Nielsen, 2017).

Bringing podcasts to the teaching of writing is a wonderful way to engage students in a timely and innovative multimodal literacy practice. Teaching the podcast may be tied to any topic instead of to more traditional research or the argument paper or as an assessment tool in response to reading or to a broader unit of study. The podcast involves the same skills and analytical approaches to research required for many state and district standards but can feel more relevant and enticing than a traditional research paper. The podcast blends research, scriptwriting, music, voice performance, and editing. You can learn a great deal about this genre by inviting a fruitful conversation with your students about their connection to it. You get a read on students' prior knowledge regarding the genre along with their insight into how the genre is evolving in real time by asking students what podcasts they listen to or have heard about.

You can immerse students in this genre by listening to various currently trending podcasts appropriate for adolescent audiences. My favorite podcasts include "The Daily" from the *New York Times*, a 20-minute podcast sharing current news and perspective. The National Public Radio (NPR) podcast series "This I Believe" and Common-Sense Media's list of "The 10 Must-Listen Podcasts for Tweens and Teens" are wonderful resources. It also helps to find examples of podcasts that fit the topic and focus of the kind of podcast you want students to create. Both NPR and the *New York Times* hold student podcast competitions and share winning and high-achieving submissions online. These make lovely model texts, as they are high-quality, thoughtful, and successfully executed podcasts created by students at the secondary level. You can gather a collection of two to three podcasts to share or have students find examples of podcasts related to their topics. As students explore and engage with model texts, they expand their writing repertoire and learn practices for approaching new types of writing rather than simply looking for a list of rules or a formula to follow.

Through analysis of models, students learn the rules and possibilities of the genre. Students need to be exposed to successful student podcasts and professional podcasts, to instill confidence that creating podcasts of their own is within reach. At the end of this chapter, I've listed some recommended sites for finding model texts.

Assignment Details

The podcast may be assigned as an individual project where each student creates their own or as a group project if the podcast lends itself to group work (pairs or small groups). Keeping the time limit requirement relatively short (5–10 minutes) works best when students work independently. If you want students to work in groups, they can create a longer podcast (10 minutes for a group of two and 20–30(ish) minutes for a group of four. If possible, keep the groups small (three to four students). Anything more significant makes the managing of roles and contributions unwieldy. It also helps to break down the podcasts' teaching, writing, and production into tangible steps.

A podcast unit typically includes the following steps:

1. Understanding the genre expectations (see reading connection section of this chapter)
2. Researching
3. Structuring a podcast: evaluating model texts, outlining
4. Podcast scripting
5. Technology and style in podcasting
6. Recording
7. Editing
8. Reflecting
9. Sharing/celebrating/publishing

As with many of the genres in this book, you want to give students a topic for their podcasts that provides enough room for them to have agency and choice in what they decide to write about. For example, students may create podcasts on current issues or events, on topics they are deeply invested in and want others to know about, or on some aspect or realm of education they want to see changed. It is also popular to participate in fandom and young adult literature, popular culture, social media, and many more. You have endless options for the assignment's focus and can make it fit the direction of your curriculum and context. At my university, my colleague and I assigned first-year college students to create podcasts about their transition to the university (Saidy, 2018). In my writing project Summer Institute with K–12 teachers, I asked teachers to create podcasts about educational issues they care deeply about. I have asked students to create podcasts about a community-embedded subject they are invested in (see Sample Podcast Assignment at the end of the chapter). Students choose a range of topics such as homelessness, clean drinking water, body image, lack of green spaces, and funding for libraries. Two teachers in my writing project, a sixth-grade teacher and a 12th-grade teacher, have their students create podcasts around social issues. In Justin's sixth-grade class, one of his sixth-graders started her podcast on the topic of immigration. In Heidi's 12th-grade class, one of her students created a podcast on the topic of birth control. (You can find both in the Sample Student Podcasts at the end of the chapter.)

I typically assign podcasts that involve making an argument and conducting research. However, there are a variety of subgenres within the broader podcast genre to choose from. This includes the following: including the podcast interview, narrative (fiction or nonfiction), conversation or panel discussion, repurposed content (contains the same message as other podcasts or texts but is delivered in a new way), or a hybrid show (a show that includes a monologue and then a conversation or panel discussion or interview. It helps to choose which of these kinds of podcasts you want students to create so you can help them navigate the necessary deliverables in creating that form of a podcast.

It is also essential to convey to students how a story can be an argument. For example, a teacher in my writing project summer institute wrote a podcast script about his life as a teacher navigating the challenges of raising a family on a teacher's salary and learning to understand how to do what he loves and earn a solid paycheck. He uses his personal story to argue against the perception that teachers are poor or that the teaching career is not a reputable or steady pathway. He weaves his narrative with external sources to support his claims.

Reading Connection

As consumers of podcasts, we listen instead of reading. Many of our students are familiar with this genre; however, they may not know the skills and strategies to listen effectively. Listening is an anchor standard of the Common Core, and even in states that have not adopted Common Core standards, they include listening in their curriculum standards. We want students to learn how to listen carefully, a core literacy skill, and understand how listening is an essential part of communicating and a crucial part of reading successfully. This includes carefully listening to this text form in the same way we ask them to read analog texts. Students may have listening habits they've formed as consumers of this genre or as consumers of other forms of social media. You can ask them to share these tips and strategies by creating a list on the whiteboard or chart paper and then adding it as they gain more. You can also share professional tips from people who make or produce podcasts. As an example, the piece in *Medium* written by Curtis Stanier (2020), "8 Tips I Use to More Effectively Learn from Podcasts," outlines specific strategies that help listeners consume podcasts in ways that work for them.

Tips range from finding the right time and space to listen to taking notes as a listening strategy. He also shares how most podcasts have something called "show notes," which are summaries of the discussion in the show. These may include references to the sources used for shared information, a show's transcript, or hyperlinks to vast resources. Some show notes include direct links to articles and books connected to the topic.

You can help students practice effective podcast listening by responding to a series of questions as they listen to their collection of models:

- What are the genre elements of a podcast?
- What are some of the elements of spoken language that seem important?
- How might you modify your text to make it a spoken text?
- Who is the audience for these spoken pieces?
- What parts of the episode are interesting? Boring? Why?
- How is the podcast structured? What do the creators do at the beginning, at the end, and during transitions?
- How does it make its argument if there is one? What rhetorical strategies does it use?
- What is the main idea or insight the podcast shares? What sound effects, music, and other tools does it use, and for what effect?
- What else do you notice?

Through close listening and analysis, students can determine what works, what doesn't, and why.

Once students have a topic, they need time to conduct research and read to inform their scriptwriting (two to eight sources depending on the length of the podcast and if they are working in groups or individually). You can have them create a brief annotated bibliography or annotated notecard (using physical notecards or in Google Docs) to track these sources and take notes on how they want to use them in the podcast. Figure 7.1 is an example of a notecard format a sixth-grade teacher in Arizona, Ginette Rossi, uses with her students.

The primary advice is to help direct students in their podcast research toward becoming astute participants. You want them to (1) find enough information on the topic that they feel they can write about it or discuss it with relative ease, (2) collect multiple perspectives on the topic so the pod-

Source 1

| Author: |
| Title: |
| Year: |
| Pages: |

☐ Article
☐ Book
☐ Website : enter hyperlink

Brief description of the main thrust of the source. 10 sentence or 150 word maximum.

FIGURE 7.1 **Annotation Notecard**

cast represents a range of opinions or lenses, and (3) give credit to external sources within the written podcast script with statements like, "According to an article written by _____ in the *Atlantic Monthly* . . ." Students need guidance in learning to embed research into their podcasts to tell their stories or form their arguments.

Writing Workshop Tip: Scriptwriting

As students gather and read external sources, they can hone their focus or argument before scriptwriting. Here are a series of reflection questions to help them think about their investment in the topic and the main idea, argument, or message they hope to convey to their audience.

Finding Focus for Your Podcast

1. What is your topic, and why do you care about it?
2. What are the root causes of this issue?
3. What is making the issue worse? What could make it better?
4. Now that you've started to think about your position on this topic, articulate your opinions as an argument. Draw from some of the facts you read or heard in your group work.
5. Keep it simple.

As students focus their arguments, they can begin scriptwriting. You can provide a podcast script writing template to help students plan and draft the different elements of their podcasts (see Table 7.2: Podcast Script Template). The template is just a suggestion for including elements but should not be used as a formula. The details may appear in the podcast in a different order, or an element may not apply and could be left out.

TABLE 7.2 **Podcast Script Template**

Time (seconds or minutes)	Script
	Opening Music and Sound Effects
	Introduction: Set the stage for your episode. • This should be 3–5 minutes. • Identify yourself and all members of the podcast (names and grades and your investment in or connection to the topic). • Tell why your show has come into being and what you hope it offers, and what the listener can expect in this show.
	Segue: Use music, sound, or a brief phrase to transition or move the piece forward.
	Main Idea or Argument and Topic Background: You might also discuss the background or relevance of the topic and define the problem or issue if there is one. Include your main point and one or two supporting details (e.g., data or quotes to back you up).
	Segue: Use music, sound, or a brief phrase to transition or move the piece forward.
	Support for Argument with Story Example, Interview, or Data **Note:** If you have a guest, plan out the interview questions so the guest knows what to expect and say.
	Segue: Use music, sound, or a brief phrase to transition or move the piece forward.
	Opinion(s): Share your perspective, thoughts, and opinions about the topic along with the perspectives of others. Do not hold back. Be honest and be you. Be sure to provide a diversity of views along with your own.
	Closing: Summarize the episode, share major takeaways and why they matter, offer a call to action and a simple sign-off or goodbye.
	Closing Music and Sound Effects or Fade Out

Total Time: _____

Be sure to have students read their scripts as a part of their editing and revision process to listen for places they stumble or places that seem unclear. The more they practice reading the scripts aloud, the more successful their recordings will be. You also want to have them time themselves to make sure the writing is clear, easy to read, and falls within the allotted time frame. You can review their podcast scripts before they record to get a sense that everyone has what they need to succeed and that the script follows the key genre elements you are assessing.

Digital Tools

Students just need a microphone, a free online account, and the internet. Audio tools are easily accessible and free, which is important in thinking and planning for equity and inclusion in the writing classroom. The easiest way for students to record the audio is with Audacity, GarageBand (available only for Mac and Apple devices), or Anchor, which are free applications for recording, editing, and publishing podcasts. Students may download and use these apps on smartphones, tablets, or other digital devices. These are all user-friendly and easy to work within the classroom. There are also YouTube tutorials on how to use each of these, which are helpful to show or make accessible for students and in case you feel less tech-savvy. Most devices have integrated microphones, which work well. If students have access to an internet-connected Chromebook, laptop, or mobile device, they are set to record their audio.

Almost all learning management services, like Blackboard and Canvas, which many schools have for organizing and sharing class curriculum and grading, have a recording component students can use. Because of the quiet required to record a high-quality podcast, students should record outside of the classroom in a quiet and controlled setting. You can ask the librarian if there are spaces available in the library for students to record or have students record in quiet nooks and crannies of the school.

After recording, it's time for students to edit their audio. You want to encourage students to record their audio chronologically in conjunction with their scripts. Sometimes they mess up a particular part and need to rerecord and splice and clip to fix it. Their first step is to arrange the audio in order and then trim and cut any mistakes, pauses, or interruptions. Next, they can add music and sound effects. If they have access to Macbooks and

GarageBand, they can easily mix music loops into their audio recordings. Audacity users cannot compose music within the software, so they need to find music elsewhere to include. Students may want to use their favorite music clips for their podcasts. Students appreciate having time in class to listen and choose music that fits. This is part of curating a multimodal text, and the music and editing choices are just as important as the scriptwriting in forming a polished podcast.

You should tell your students that any recordings they use need to be "Podsafe," which is an informal term that means legal to distribute online for others to listen to and download freely. There are many sites that purport to offer Podsafe music, but the students have to be careful to read the terms of use on any such site to make sure that the site promises that the recordings being offered there are actually being offered with their owners' permission (see the Author's Note on copyright and terms of use).

Extensions

We want students to celebrate what they've accomplished when they have finished editing their podcasts. There are many fun ways to extend the podcast unit by finding audiences and purposes for students to share their work beyond the classroom community. One of the ways to do this is to have a podcast listening party. You can set up listening stations around the room (laptops or tablets with headphones) and have students rotate from one podcast to another and leave feedback on sticky notes for the authors. You can extend the podcast listening party to include family and friends and hold a public exhibition of podcasts where students' podcasts are linked to QR codes; students may invite guests to include family and support figures from their lives, or you can invite other classes to attend (Guggenheim, Glover, & Mejia, 2021). You can also have students create podcasts connected to student podcast contests or challenges and then, at the end of the unit, submit them to these publication venues.

PODCAST MODEL TEXTS: SOME PLACES TO FIND THEM

Storycorps: https://storycorps.org/

Science Friday: https://www.sciencefriday.com/science-friday-podcasts/

Youth Radio Media: https://yr.media/

iTunes Free Podcast Library: https://podcasts.apple.com/us/genre/podcasts/id26

This I Believe: https://thisibelieve.org/podcasts/

Radio Rookies: https://www.wnyc.org/shows/rookies/

Common Sense Media: The 10 Must-Listen Podcasts for Tweens and Teens: https://www.commonsensemedia.org/blog/10-must-listen-podcasts-for-tweens-and-teens

NPR Student Podcast Challenge: https://www.npr.org/2018/11/15/650500116/npr-student-podcast-challenge-home

PODCAST SAMPLE ASSIGNMENT: CREATE A PODCAST FOR POSITIVE CHANGE!

Description:

For this project, I am asking you to investigate the following question: What is a problem or issue in your community that you want to see change for the better or you want people to understand in a new light? Explain the issue and a solution or the issue and the way you want people to see it differently.

To answer this question, I want you to create a podcast in Adobe Audition to teach others about the issue and advocate for positive change in connection to the issue. This is an audio text, but you will create a written script before recording.

In creating your podcast, I ask that you employ the techniques of effective podcasting we have learned about in this unit. Your podcast should include a compelling introduction, a clear argument, story or information to back up your argument, quotes from interview(s), and background music and sound effects where appropriate. In particular, draw on the example podcasts from this unit to consider how you can use your podcast to impact your community positively.

Audience: You will share this podcast with the class at a final podcast listening gallery. I would also like you to consider sending your podcast to a local podcast publishing space.

Requirements:

- Record a 5–7 minute podcast created using Anchor.
- Explain the topic and its relevance to your audience.
- Integrate appropriate and relevant research to back up your ideas (scholarly sources, statistics, newspaper articles, etc.).
- Create a works cited list including three citations, following MLA requirements.
- Use appropriate music, sound effects, etc., to make your podcast.
- The final draft should be polished, and you should make significant changes from the first draft to the final.

PODCAST SAMPLE ASSIGNMENT *CONTINUED*

Due Dates:

- Topic, three sources (10 points) ___
- Opening one to two paragraphs of podcast script (20 points) ___
- Script outline (20 points) ___
- Draft of works cited list (20 points) ___
- Recording draft due to Dropbox (20 points) ___
- Conference (10 points) ___ and ___
- Final draft and works cited (150 points) ___

*Your rough draft may be submitted in MP3 or MP4 on Canvas.

*Final podcast must be submitted via Anchor. Works cited list must be submitted via Canvas.

PODCAST SCRIPT STUDENT EXAMPLE 1

Sixth-Grade Student

Podcast Topic: Immigration

Time	Script
25 seconds	[Podcast opens with powerful inspirational quote or sound bite] [Then fades slowly]
10 seconds	"Hello, my name is Natalia, the host of today's podcast. With me is my guest Delmy, owner-operator of a McDonald's franchise in Austin, Texas. She is also known as my tía."
20 seconds	Today we will be talking about immigration. Specifically, about the hard work, determination, and how immigrants contribute to our society. We'll talk about how immigrants are changing our nation every single day. How dependent we are on immigrants for many of our needs.
7 seconds	[sad violin]
11 minutes and 10 seconds	We will begin with hearing from Delmy. Now Delmy, tell me how old you were when you came? [she answers] How did you feel when you first went to school? [she responds] I say something thoughtful and move on to the next question. What was the most difficult or scariest part of coming into a new country? [she answers] What was your favorite part of being in a new country? [she responds] How did you get to where you are today in your business? [she answers] About how many people are employed at your McDonald's? [she answers] Do you work with any charities, and if so, why? What was the hardest thing you had to overcome? [she answers] Do you think that immigrants today are treated with respect? [she answers] What advice do you have for Latinas and Latinos? [she answers]
12 seconds	Thank you for doing the interview. You are a great role model for Latina girls like me. And you give hope and courage to many immigrants. Thank you for giving back to this country that is now your home.
25 seconds	The article, "Key Findings about US Immigrants," from Pew Research states that "In 2017, about 29 million immigrants were working or looking for work in the US, making up some 17% of the total civilian labor force. Lawful immigrants made up most of the immigrant workforce, at 21.2 million." This is a huge amount of our population being immigrants that do a ton of our work. We should all be thankful for their hard work and their devotion.

PODCAST SCRIPT STUDENT EXAMPLE 1 *CONTINUED*

Time	Script
1 minute and 10 seconds	Have you ever heard of "the Dreamers"? If not, see the article on the *America's Voice* blog titled, "Immigration 101: What is a Dreamer?" The article states that Dreamer "refers to an immigrant youth who qualifies for the Development, Relief, and Education for Alien Minors (DREAM) Act . . . . The Dream Act is a piece of legislation first introduced to Congress in 2001 that would create a pathway to citizenship for young people who were brought to the United States as children without documentation. These are young people who are American in every way, except on paper. They have grown up in this country and consider themselves to be American but lack the documents to fully engage in the country they call home."
41 seconds	Now let's focus on how immigrants give back to the United States. An article called "Immigrants Contribute Greatly to the US Economy, Despite Administration's 'Public Charge' Rule Rationale" published by the Center for Budget & Policy Priorities states that, immigrants "work at high rates and make up more than a third of the workforce in some industries."
5 seconds	Thank you for listening, and I hope you enjoyed it. I hope I have taught you something about immigration in the United States.

Total Time: 14:45

PODCAST SCRIPT STUDENT EXAMPLE 2

Twelfth-Grade Student

Podcast Topic: Birth Control

[Opening music jingle and sound effects]

Intro: Setting the Stage

"Hello, this is Avery's Podcast. I'm your host, Avery, and today we're going to talk about birth control. We will talk about how it works and what to expect when using it—with my mom, Suzanne."

"Suzanne is a mother of three. Today she is going to share with us some of her experience on using birth control and, more specifically, on what she has learned while using the pill."

Topic 1: Lack of Education

1. There is a huge lack of education on birth control and because of this, there is a stigma surrounding using it. It is too often frowned upon and I hear too many college students, who are my age, saying it shouldn't be used.

2. Because of misinformation and social stigma, many teen girls and women are scared to start using it or are scared of people finding out that they use it.

3. I am a teen girl who uses birth control and this can sometimes be difficult socially. There are people out there who like to make assumptions about me and my body. They make assumptions about why I'm on it and about my values. I try not to care about what they say. I know why I am taking birth control, and my close friends know why. That's all I need. Sometimes it's tough, though.

Segue (can be a sound effect, short musical clip, or a phrase)

Topic 2: Birth Control—what it does and what options are available

1. Birth control does not just prevent pregnancy. It can help acne, cramps, period regulation, heaviness of flow, and much more. It can help women be in control of their own bodies.

2. There are many forms of birth control, and some are used for different reasons. For example, if your doctor gives you the okay, you can take the pill continuously to stop you from menstruating altogether. This

can be helpful for women athletes or others who feel burden by their
period every month.

3. Birth control comes in various forms. It can come in the form of IUDs,
two kinds of pills, an injection, an implant, and a patch. Each form does
relatively the same thing, but the side effects and benefits vary.

4. According to the blog, "The Vote & the Right to Access" on the site
The Power to Decide, "The Food and Drug Administration approved
the birth control pill, which allowed many women to plan if, when, and
under what circumstances to get pregnant and have a child" (Power to
Decide, 2019).

Topic 3: Myths

1. There are a lot of myths surrounding birth control. Some people think it
is unhealthy to be on it for an extended period of time or that it messes
with your fertility. Others think you cannot get pregnant right after
getting off of it and that your body needs breaks from the hormones.

2. Many doctors and researchers have spoken up about these myths and
have denied every single claim. It is only unhealthy to be getting the
shot for more than two years because it is stored in your bone marrow
and could cause bone decay; it does not mess with your fertility; and
you can get pregnant immediately off birth control.

3. Scientific research has proven that weight gain, fertility issues, toler-
ance breaks, and taking it at the exact time every day so it'll work are
all false claims. As long as you take your birth control every day, these
things will not be an issue.

4. According to the Simple Health's, which is a birth control company,
website, "Hormonal contraception is a powerful medication, but it
is safe to use indefinitely." "Whether you've been on the pill for one
month or fifteen years, you can get pregnant after you stop taking it."

Closing remarks/recap:

"This podcast has been interesting, and I enjoyed hearing about your
experience! I hope this podcast was helpful to you and that you may
have learned something. Thank you for joining me and talking about birth
control with me, Mom."

[Closing music jingle/sound effect]

References

Buzzsprout. How to structure your podcast in 4 steps. https://www.buzzsprout
.com/blog/podcast-structure

Guggenheim, A., Glover, D. & Mejia., A. G. (2021). Voices and sounds heard:
Composing through narrative podcasting. *English Journal, 110*(4), 37–44.

Jones, Leigh A. (2010). Podcasting and performativity: Multimodal invention
in an advanced writing class. *Composition Studies, 38*(2), 75–91.

The Nielsen Company. (2017). Nielsen podcast insights. https://www.nielsen
.com/us/en/insights/report/2017/nielsen-podcast-insights-q3-2017/

PPL PRS United for Music. (2021). The growing popularity of podcasts.
https://pplprs.co.uk/popularity-of-podcasts/

Saidy, C. (2018). Beyond words on the page: Using multimodal composing
to aid in the transition to first-year writing. *Teaching English in the Two-
Year College, 45*(3), 255–272.

Selfe, Cynthia L. (2009). The movement of air, the breath of meaning: Aural-
ity and multimodal composing. *College Composition and Communication,
60*(4), 616–663.

Winn, R. (2021). 2021 podcast stats and facts. https://www.podcastinsights
.com/podcast-statistics

CHAPTER 8

The Proposal

A semester does not go by when I haven't written a proposal for one reason or another. I write course proposals to create new courses, conference proposals to share my research and teaching, and grant proposals to seek funding for my research and community-embedded outreach. My husband, who is an artist, writes proposals to the city for competitions for funding for public art projects. In many careers, such as marketing, advertising, and development, you are required to create proposals or pitches to gain new clients. Proposal writing can also be part of living in a community as an active and engaged citizen. For example, much to my chagrin, if I want to paint or make changes to the appearance of my house in the neighborhood, I must write a proposal to the neighborhood association for approval of this work. Or, if a community organization or neighborhood association wants to make changes to the city, like adding speed bumps to slow traffic or creating bike lanes for alternative transportation routes, these changes must be proposed formally through the city council. Proposals serve to communicate ideas, create teams and plans, and secure funding and support for work in the world. As teachers of writing, we can give our students practice writing this genre to help prepare them to learn to communicate their ideas, to contribute to their communities, and to think about the ways they can make a difference in the lives of others.

When I listen to my students' conversations that reveal their stresses and obsessions, I am constantly struck by their investment and interest in issues within and beyond their communities. They have just lived through a global pandemic and #BlackLivesMatter and are bombarded daily with the realities of global warming. They have also witnessed the way people have made a difference in small and huge ways in the world and in their own lives through innovative ideas and activism. They have big topics on their minds and need ways of extending their understanding, thinking of solutions, and giving voice to their ideas. By embedding proposal writing into your curriculum, you can give students an avenue to voice their ideas and to imagine ways to make change in their communities and beyond. Writing a community-embedded proposal is an opportunity to have students think outside the box, turn to look at their communities (neighborhood, city, state) and think of a concrete and tangible way to affect change. This project prepares students for their professional, academic, and civic futures by providing an opportunity to practice their skills in teamwork, leadership, project development, business plan creation, public speaking, and network creation. They also become prepared to enter additional competitions for business plans and innovative projects for youth if these are available in their communities.

Assignment Details

There are different varieties of proposals operating in the world, including research proposals, business proposals, grant proposals, conference proposals, proposal letters, and more. The kind of proposal assignment I use most often with students is a community-embedded action proposal, which I call the Changemaker Proposal. It has all the makings of a community-embedded grant proposal and serves as a way for students to bring their ideas and interests to their writing with the support of a clear genre framework to guide them.

The Changemaker Proposal assignment is a proposal to create positive and actionable change in their communities. It addresses the following genre elements:

1. Identifies a compelling need and presents a clear solution to a local challenge (in a community you are a part of)

2. Explains why this idea is innovative or bold
3. Shares the potential for this project or plan to grow or to be sustained
4. Describes the ways the project can be sustained over time
5. Explains how you can measure the impact of this project on the community or some part of the community
6. Details how the idea will happen
7. Provides a clear and detailed budget using $2,500 as your total award
8. Provides a clear feasible timeline for the accomplishment of the project (This can be a calendar with key action items)
9. Addresses any risks and challenges and how you will overcome them

You can have students write their proposals as grant-like written narratives or as digital presentations. Either way, it is useful to provide headings to support their writing. Most proposals for grants or competitions have these kinds of parameters and guidelines clearly listed for writers to follow so they can provide the information needed for the specific audience and purpose (see Changemaker Proposal Assignment Guidelines).

I often assign the proposal as a research and writing project for midsemester or end of semester. I formally introduce the project a few weeks before the scheduled midterm or final for the class and have students present their projects in lieu of a final exam. You can teach this any time of the year that works for your curriculum and can pair it with reading of books of choice connected to activism and changemaking or to a book you are reading that connects in some way thematically. The proposal project can be completed individually or as a group project. If a group project, it is important to take the time for teams to work together to come up with a community-embedded action project that all team members are invested in and want to contribute to equally. Then it is essential to help students in dividing tasks.

One of the challenges of teaching this genre is that it is often hidden from public view. Proposals are typically circulated within specific communities for very specific purposes, and they remain within those spaces. Proposals often count as the behind-the-scenes work that leads to a public project or a published piece or a change of some kind. The proposal itself is usually read by an editorial team or judging panel or governing body and is not on display for all to see. This can make proposals tough to access. However, this is more reason to teach this genre. Whenever possible, we want to make visible the invisible yet critical kinds of writing that take place in the world. Whenever I find a genre that I want to teach that fits this category of hidden from public view, I take this as a challenge and go on a hunt to find it. You can do this by asking people you know who write proposals for their work to share them with you. You can share examples of your own writing, and you can start uncovering the genre in places you didn't know it existed. Once you teach proposal writing, you also want to save (with permission) examples of student work so you can use these as models in future semesters or years (see for example the Student Changemaker Proposal at the end of this chapter). When you take the time to look at proposals with students, you can start to break down the genre by looking at the common elements. You can show students how writing is rarely pure in its rhetorical mode. Good proposals use analogy, arguments, and narrative; they weave in and out of patterns of development and modes of writing. This strengthens the work overall.

Connection to Reading

One of the ways to connect proposal writing to reading in the beginning of the project, when students are brainstorming community-embedded action ideas, is to give them examples of what is possible. You can collect articles about other young adults committed to creating positive change in their communities. For example, in my community in Tempe, Arizona, a recent article described an event where youth activists were asked to remove political messaging from their faces at a diversity award ceremony. They had written messages to raise awareness about climate change and they refused to remove the writing (*AZ Republic*, 2020). Another article describes how youth activists approached our state senator, Krysten Sinema, to protest her stance on immigration. The article describes the work of these young activists to hold politicians accountable for creating pathways to citizenship (Cortez, 2021). You can find resources for students to turn to connected to your local context. There are also resources such as Naomi Klein's (2021), *How to Change Everything*, a collection of chapters on young adult changemakers working on climate activism, or the Born This Way Foundation and Lady Gaga's *Channel Kindness: Stories of Kindness and Community*, a collection of stories of young people who started their own social movements or change projects. There are also TED talks with young activists sharing their work, like Samuel Caruso's TED talk, "The Future is Ours: Student Activism," about overcoming hopelessness through his work as a teen activist fighting for gun control in his community and beyond. These texts served as resources for students to generate ideas about what they care about in their communities and to see what changemaking and societal impacts are possible at their age.

CHANGEMAKER MODEL TEXTS: SOME PLACES TO FIND THEM

1. Portland Public Library Teen: Activists & Activism
2. Powell's Books
3. KQED Youth Activism Newsela Articles
4. Chicago Public Library Social Justice Books for Teens
5. School Library Journal: A Roundup of Books on Activism, Social Justice, and Histories of Protest
6. The Teach Thought website's Teaching Social Justice: 25 Books to Encourage Students to Change the World

You may give students access to a variety of changemaker texts so they can have examples from a diverse array of perspectives. You can select excerpts for them to read or have them choose texts to read as a complementary book choice reading assignment to go along with the project proposal. Whether you take either approach, there are rich resources for finding diverse collections of stories about youth and adult changemakers in the world.

A continual aim during the proposal brainstorming and drafting stages is to saturate students with information about and models of successful adolescent changemakers in action. You can assign students a couple of the chapters or whole books to read in class and for homework. You may also partner with your school librarian to order or make available a cart of books on teen changemakers to use as a classroom resource for students to gather ideas and inspiration from other young activists. You can invite students to collect articles from recent websites or news outlets that tell stories of young activists. You can also inform students of local events, films, and author readings about activist issues. Through these examples, students are reminded that this kind of dedication and interest often grows out of everyday experience. Once students are immersed in examples, you can have them start brainstorming ideas for their own proposal projects.

It is helpful to give them a way to step back from the examples they read to think about the project ideas of individual changemakers and the steps they took to accomplish them. You can do this by asking students to collect information on the changemakers as they dive into reading, whether

CHANGEMAKER MODEL TEXTS

assigned in class or done as choice reading outside of class, or both. You can have them gather this information in a simple table (see Table 8.1: Tracking the Work of Changemakers).

TABLE 8.1 **Tracking the Work of Changemakers**

Title of text read	
Name of changemaker	
Project idea	
Strategy	
Timeline	
Support and obstacles	
Outcome	
Impact	

Once students have read about changemakers out in the world, you can have them share what they have learned through a Changemaker Tea Party. The tea party is an idea I have adapted from Linda Christensen's (2017), *Reading, Writing, and Rising Up*. Have students choose one of the changemakers they have read about and get in character as this person for a tea party exchange. Every student gets in character as an individual changemaker, and they go around the room meeting and greeting other changemakers. The goal is to learn about a diverse array of people doing work to influence

CONTINUED

positive change, to show off what they have learned through their reading, and to have fun.

Research

Along with reading examples of youth activists and sample proposals, you want to have students conduct enough research on their project topics to make informed and actionable proposals. You can ask students to read external sources (how many sources depends on grade level and time) to gain a sense of the issue they want to address, who the main players are who are already working on this issue, and different perspectives and strategies for implementing change. Here is a series of steps you can have students take in the reading and research process to help inform their proposal writing. You can do this through a research organizer (see Research Organizer for Proposal Writing).

Taking students through the steps of conducting research to find current news, local or national organizations, and two people connected to their topic gives them firsthand experience with multiple forms of research and information. They may synthesize information and apply it to their own ideas and thinking, and they get to explore work being done out in the world connected to issues that matter to them. They also make connections with people in their communities doing work that they admire, people they want to learn from. They gain experience with primary and secondary sources while building a case for their own project plans.

RESEARCH ORGANIZER FOR PROPOSAL WRITING

Step 1: In the News

Use an online news source of your choice to find an article connected to your issue. You can choose a local news article that is directly tied to your topic, or a regional or national news article that is related to your issue but is in a different location.

Please respond to the following questions in response to the news article you find:

1. What is the article source information (name of the newspaper, title of article, author, publication date, and website address to locate article)?
2. What is the issue or problem described in the article?
3. Who is impacted by the issue? List all people affected.
4. What was the solution implemented to help solve the problem? Did it work?
5. How was the project implemented? How long did it take? What did it cost?
6. Were there any obstacles faced by the implementation? Explain.
7. How does this article relate to your project proposal plan? What do you take away from it that you can apply to your own project plan?

Step 2: Local or National Organization

Conduct an online search for a nonprofit or government organization that does work to address the problem you have identified.

1. List the name of the organization and website address and where they are located. Are they local or national or both?
2. What are their goals? How do they address the problem you are trying to solve?
3. What resources do they have that could help inform your work?

Step 3: Changemakers, Teen or Adult

Find two adults you think can help you in some way to impact change related to your issue. It is wonderful if these people live within your community, but they don't have to. You just need relatively easy access to communicate with them in some way. You may already know this person and they can be a relative, neighbor, or friend. They may do work connected to this issue or have resources or expertise about it.

Changemaker #1

1. Name
2. Job title or position in the community
3. How do you think this person can be of help to you in connection with your project?
4. Why would this person want to work with and support you?
5. Contact information

Changemaker #2

1. Name
2. Job title or position in community
3. How do you think this person can be of help to you in connection with your project?
4. Why would this person want to work with and support you?
5. Contact information

Writing Workshop: Mini Lessons on Proposal Planning

Writing workshop days during a proposal writing unit may cover a number of different topics. You could use this time to invite students to write, discuss, and reflect on defining and narrowing their issue. Or, they could focus on proposing a solution that is feasible and attractive to their audience. One workshop could teach students to employ the classical rhetorical appeals effectively in their writing. Throughout these workshops, students can discuss their ideas and share their writing in pairs, trios, or small groups. While students are writing or researching, it helps to conference with each student about their individual projects several times throughout the course of the project to make sure they are on track and that they have selected a topic that is realistic. One of the ways to help students plan their projects and break each step down is by using a proposal-planning document (see Table 8. 3).

RESEARCH ORGANIZER FOR PROPOSAL WRITING

TABLE 8.3 **Proposal-Planning Document**

Directions: Submit this planning document with the final draft of your proposal so I can see your planning process.

1. What is the problem or issue you want to address in your community?	2. What is your personal connection to this issue or community?
3. What is your proposed solution?	4. Why or how do you know it will work?
5. Who will be the audience for your proposal? Why or how do they have the power to change this issue?	6. Why would the community benefit from your project?

CONTINUED

7. How will you use your funding to implement the project? Break down your expenses and explain.	8. What is your timeline?
9. What evidence or information will help make a case for why your project matters and can make an impact? (Include sources.)	

You can break the writing process down into tangible steps by having students work on one section of the proposal at a time.

Digital Tools

Proposal writing lends itself perfectly to the use of digital tools. In fact, one way to teach the proposal is to have students create a multimodal final proposal document. A multimodal text is constructed using multiple modes of representation and communication such as writing, images, recording or voice-over, or video. You can share models of multimodal composition so students have examples of what this kind of writing looks like to help them

RESEARCH ORGANIZER FOR PROPOSAL WRITING

conceptualize their project. There are wonderful multimodal texts to choose as composition models, like "What Happened to You" and "Oak Flat" (both nonfiction multimodal texts). Students can create an Adobe Spark page. Adobe Spark supports multimodal composing. The Adobe Spark platform is a way to share a proposal and make an argument using images, words, sounds, multiple languages, and links. Students can compose in multimodal forms with intentional design.

Extensions

One of the gifts of a proposal writing unit is that students begin projects that often continue. For example, one of my high school students in years past created a proposal for a mural project at the school to celebrate diversity. In her proposal, she created a sample section of the mural, which was a painting that would become part of a larger mural design for the school. She shared her proposal with the art department and administration to design and complete her mural, which she did by the end of her senior year. One of my high school seniors, after creating a poster and a wealth of talking points on the issue of animal testing and mistreatment, became part of the larger animal rights movement, taking part in teach-ins and demonstrations. Students demonstrated and experienced political imagination turned into action that went beyond the parameters of the classroom assignment and into their lives as young activists and changemakers.

One of the ways to celebrate the work of proposal writing is to have students share their proposals in the form of a project pitch. You can have them prepare a 3-minute presentation in which they share the gist of their proposal plans with the class. This gives students an opportunity to practice sharing their ideas with others and communicating their arguments orally, which is often part of the proposal process. You can have students share their proposals using Adobe Spark, PowerPoint, Google Slides, or whatever digital tool fits your context. Here are some tips to help students think about selling their proposal ideas in a brief pitch to their peers:

CONTINUED

Developing Your Pitch

- Tell a story. What is your connection to this proposal plan?
- Be focused and keep your pitch simple.
- Make every pitch a visual journey. Use images and infographics or music.
- Make a strong early impression (i.e., cover slide on both pitch decks and informal pitches).
- Leave time for questions.

Another way to extend this work is to look for funding opportunities in your local area where students could send their proposals, if they choose to try to get them funded. There are local community organizations like churches, Boys and Girls Clubs, and colleges and universities that are seeking innovative projects from youth. There are also national and international organizations such as the Youth and Education Grant-Making Program, the W. K. Kellogg Foundation, and Ashoka, that have funding streams for youth activism projects.

Teaching proposal writing gives students a foundation and tools necessary to launch out of the classroom and into the worlds of professional, academic, and civic life. Equally important, this work builds bridges from one student to another. They learn about one another's passions and ideas and they grow compassion for each other, not just for causes outside of themselves. Students become one another's teachers and support each other's ideas, edit one another's pieces, and witness challenges and successes.

SAMPLE ASSIGNMENT FOR PROPOSAL WRITING: CHANGEMAKER PROPOSAL TEMPLATE

Instructions: Use this template to write your proposal in no more than eight pages with a 12-point font. Upload your completed proposal as a PDF to our class Canvas page [place your school's link here].

Purpose: In this proposal, you will examine a societal problem of interest, then develop a solution via a research-based proposal argument. Instead of focusing solely on reacting to the problem, this project asks you to develop actionable measures to, over time, solve the problem by means of an innovative and creative solution.

> **PROJECT TITLE**
>
> > AUDIENCE: Community-Embedded Funding Source (what individual or group do you think would fund this project and why?)

Project Overview

Share a summary of the community-embedded project you are proposing.

- Briefly introduce your idea for creating positive change in the community.
- Identify a compelling need and present a clear solution to a local challenge (in your community).
- Explain how your proposed project will enable or support others in the community.

Community Contributions

Share with us your thoughts on the contributions your proposed project will make to your community and beyond.

- Explain how your project will contribute to a specific part of your local community.

CONTINUED

- Discuss the potential of your project to grow and be sustained within the community.
- Describe the resource, event, or impact that will be created through your proposed project and how you will share with others.

Project Details

Expand on the details of your proposed project.

- Describe the local or regional settings where your work will occur and any connections with community or stakeholder groups. If applicable, describe how your project engages groups or organizations to promote sustained community engagement.
- Include a timeline of the major activities and milestones for your proposed project over the 12-month period of performance beginning _____ and ending _____ .
- List the team members who will be involved in the proposed project. Explain how the members of this team will contribute to this work.
- Include any challenges or obstacles that you will face and how you will overcome them.

Budget Narrative

Describe in one paragraph how the grant funds requested in the $2,500 budget contribute to the goals of creating positive change within the local community. Detail how you will budget your plan with the following categories: (1) supplies and materials and (2) stipends for individuals, food, and/or travel.

- Remember: You do not need to use all these categories. The total must equal $2,500 and not a dollar over.
- Remember: Your budget is an argument. You are making a case for how you will accomplish this work.

PROPOSAL STUDENT EXAMPLE

Ninth-Grade Student

Changemaker Proposal

PROJECT TITLE: Creating a School Mural for Equity and Inclusion

AUDIENCE: Community-embedded funding source (who or what group do you think would fund this project) and why?

I want to see if the school or school district will fund this project. If there is no money from the school or district, I plan to reach out to the PTA to see if they can help provide funding or do a fundraiser for my mural project.

Project Overview

Share a summary of the community embedded project you are proposing.

- Briefly introduce your idea for creating positive change in the community.
- Identify a compelling need and present a clear solution to a local challenge (in your community).
- Explain how your proposed project will enable or support others in the community.

My issue is discrimination. I am proposing a school-funded mural to create a more inclusive environment and message at the school. We have a compelling need here at our school to work toward better inclusivity and respect for one another. I believe the more we are surrounded by messages of acceptance and caring, the better we will act toward one another. There are far too many fights that the administration must break up each week and there are far too many kids being bullied or treated badly for their differences. We should celebrate difference and that is what my mural will focus on. The mural will be painted by students for students and will set an example of how we, as young people, can make a difference and work toward change at the local school level.

CONTINUED

Community Contributions

Share with us your thoughts on the contributions your proposed project will make to your community and beyond.

- Explain how your project will contribute to a specific part of your local community.
- Discuss the potential of your project to grow and be sustained within the community.
- Describe the resource, event, or impact that will be created through your proposed project and how you will share with others.

This project will make a drab and depressing hallway in our middle school stand out with vibrant color and creativity. This can serve as a model for ways students can imagine ideas for improving their schools and communities and make an impact one step at a time. This mural project could spread like wildfire in the district and other students at other schools may be inspired to create murals to support diversity and respect.

Project Details

Expand on the details of your proposed project.

- Describe the local or regional settings where your work will occur and any connections with community or stakeholder groups. If applicable, describe how your project engages groups or organizations to promote sustained community engagement.
- Include a timeline of the major activities and milestones for your proposed project over the 12-month period of performance beginning _____ and ending _____ .
- List the team who will be involved in the proposed project. Explain how the members of this team will contribute to this work.
- Include any challenges or obstacles that you will face and how you will overcome them.

I need to create a mock-up of my mural to show others what I am thinking in terms of design. I also need to measure the hallway space I have in mind for the painting and gain permission from officials here at my school to paint a mural on the school and, hopefully have them pay for it! Once I receive permission, I will paint one of the sections as a model. I am going to do this at home in my basement. Then, I am going to use my computer at home to draft a proposal. I will probably have my mom read it and tell me what she thinks. Then, I will send it to the administration and find out if they have any suggestions to strengthen it. I will also share my mock-up with the student government so I can get input from my peers.

My mural will take a few weeks to paint. I will recruit other students to help with the painting process and I will ask the art teacher to help if she has time. I plan to do the painting after school, so I do not interrupt classes or risk students touching the walls when the paint is wet.

Budget Narrative

Describe in one paragraph how the grant funds requested in the $2,500 budget contribute to the goals of creating positive change within the local community. Detail how you will budget your plan with the following categories: (1) supplies and materials and (2) stipends for individuals, food, and/or travel.

- Remember: You do not need to use all these categories and the total must equal $2,500 and not a dollar over.
- Remember: Your budget is an argument. You are making a case for how you will accomplish this work.

As far as a budget, I will need to have money to pay for paint (probably $350) and I may need paper to make stencils and brushes. I think I can complete this whole project for $500. I need to do more research to find out the cost of paint. I will ask the art teacher and go online to look at paint stores. My parents are also friends with an artist who creates murals for our city. I will ask him what he thinks the cost of supplies and paint will be.

References

Cortez, A. (2021). Immigration activists confront, follow Krysten Sinema to bathroom at ASU. https://www.azfamily.com

Pineda, P. (2020). Youth activists asked to remove political messaging at Tempe ceremony. They refused. https://www.azcentral.com.

Conclusion: An Invitation

This book is an invitation for secondary writing teachers to expand their view of what counts as college-ready, academic, or rigorous writing to include a diverse range of written genre forms in the secondary writing curriculum. I hope the genre selections included in these pages are ones you may take up and use in your classroom. Or that you begin to see the diverse range of genres produced around you within your school, neighborhood, community, and online and bring these into your writing curriculum.

There are endless possibilities using different genres for students to write for audiences and purposes beyond the classroom. Students can write postcards, license plates, speeches, toasts, and blogs to communicate their ideas and envision their futures. They can write book reviews and post them on Goodreads or Amazon book reviews. They may write for local or national writing invitations or competitions, such as *New York Times'* writing contests (see *New York Times* Learning Network Writing Contests). You can select from a range of national writing competitions from podcasts to profiles and involve multimodal composition. Or have students engage with KQED's Youth Media Challenges, which vary from political cartoons to writing about future political issues and elections. Students may write to participate in the Scholastic Arts and Writing Awards or local city or library writing contests. Students may write slam poetry and hold slam poetry and open mic events for their peers and families, or partner with other classes or grade levels to write for community change or for one another. You can have a high school class write children's stories for elementary age students or you can partner with another teacher and have students write across content areas.

Ultimately, our job as teachers of writing is to have our students experience the way reading and writing are tools they can use for the entirety of their lives. We want students to see how writing gives them a way to voice who we are and what we care about. They can write to advocate for change, to make sense of information and ideas, and to plan for their future lives. It is our job to give students opportunities to experience the diversity and range of writing that takes place in the world while also providing support to take risks and try the unfamiliar. We may offer model texts, strategies, and prompts for students so they do not feel overwhelmed or stopped in their tracks by unfamiliar genres or blank pages.

Teaching writing with a genre framework helps demystify the moves writers make when writing for specific audiences and purposes. The genre framework points to repeated and necessary patterns. It also helps us expand our understanding of how writing works in the world beyond modes and away from the tired and repeated patterns of five-paragraph essays and book reports. The genre framework invites us to think of writing as a social act that is grounded in context and purpose. We may use this approach to pair the teaching of writing with reading in new and creative ways. We can use reading to support writing to show model texts to understand the moves other writers make when writing a genre, to research new information, and to respond to and make sense of material.

Too often, we expect students to reach higher standards by writing impersonal or formulaic essays without enough direct engagement with or relevance to their lives. Let us instead offer students opportunities to write across a range of genres to bring who they are and what they care about to their pages. There are many ways to remix writing instruction in order to engage students with the worlds they are a part of and the ones they hope to join one day. We can tap into and extend our students' expertise with digital and multimodal communication and help them plan for their future lives by writing in innovative genres.

At the core of *Next Generation Genres* is the social nature of writing. Through this approach to teaching writing, students choose topics based on their interests, friendships, hobbies, or relationships. They can reach out to people to interview and to learn from their families and communities, and they have audiences with whom to engage and share.

The invitations in this book focus on the kinds of literacies used now in this digital age of communication that will prepare all students for their future pathways in college, the workplace, and the community. My hope is that you take up the teaching of diverse genres in whatever way best fits your students, context, curriculum requirements, and tried-and-true approaches. This book's driving force is to meet adolescents where they are and tap into what they care about and what they are interested in reading and writing. Our students will benefit from the opportunity to engage in inquiry and writing that is personal and relevant to them and to make meaningful change in their own lives and communities. I hope the suggestions in these pages will be helpful in your own journey, as you help students see themselves as writers in and out of school and you empower them to be agents of positive change.

Index

Note: Italicized page locators refer to figures; tables are noted with a *t*.

About the Author

Jessica Singer Early is a professor of English Education at Arizona State University. She is the Director of the Central Arizona Writing Project, a local site of the National Writing Project, and began her career in the field of education as a high school English Language Arts teacher in Portland, Oregon. Her research combines qualitative and quantitative methods to examine the teaching of writing and writing practices in ethnically and linguistically diverse secondary English Language Arts classrooms, as well as the preparation and professional development of urban English Language Arts teachers. Early's previous books include *Creating Literacy Communities as Pathways to Success: Equity and Access for Latina Students* (Routledge, 2018), *Real World Writing for Secondary Students: Teaching the College Admission Essay and Other Gate-Openers for Higher Education* (Teachers College Press, 2012), and *Stirring up Justice: Writing and Reading to Change the World* (Heinemann, 2006).